Cardiff Libraries
www.cardiff.gov.uk/libraries

Llyfrgelloedd Caerdyd
www.caerdydd.gov.uk/llyfrgelloe

South Glamorgan's Heritage

endpapers: St Mary Street, Cardiff, attributed to Thomas Rowlandson

frontispiece: Romano-British stone lion discovered at Cowbridge

South Glamorgan's Heritage: The Archaeology of a County

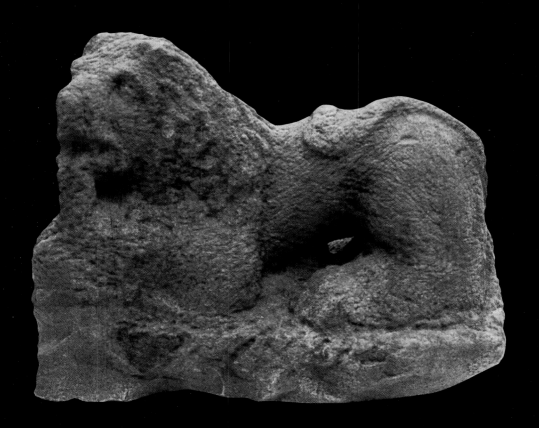

David M Robinson

The Glamorgan-Gwent Archaeological Trust

1985

Published by
The Glamorgan-Gwent Archaeological Trust Ltd

First Published 1985

ISBN 0 9506950 8 4

Designed by Sai Design, Bridgend

Printed by D Brown & Sons Ltd, Bridgend

'This part of the country was always renowned as well for the fertility of the soil, and abundance of all things serving to the necessity or pleasure of man, as also for the temperature and wholesomeness of the air. . . This, for the most part, was a plain even soil, saving for low swelling hills rising in respect of the low bottoms of vales where rivers run in, wherewith it is well replenished, which rivers, well stored with fish, plenty deep moors do compass, and near towards the plains pleasant meadows and fruitful pastures, the plains fertile and apt for tillage, bearing abundance of all kinds of grain, replenished with great store of cold sweet springs'

Rice Merrick on south Glamorgan
in *Morganiae Archaiographia*
edited by B Ll James (Barry 1983)

For friends, old and new, who listened ....
Especially Jane— δέν πειράζει, από τη λάμψη σου έγινε πραγματικό

Contents

Contents

List of Illustrations

List of Illustrations

Preface

This is by no means a definitive work; it would be impossible to do justice to the extremely rich heritage of South Glamorgan within the compass of so few pages. Rather, it is intended as a visual introduction, a mere sample to whet the appetite of perhaps an 'unsuspecting' local population. The contents stem directly from an exhibition, entitled *South Glamorgan's Heritage: Revealing the Past*, launched during October 1983 within the Canal Underpass at Kingsway, Cardiff. The exhibition was received warmly, and remained on display throughout what was nationally designated *Heritage Year* (1984). Hence, a more permanent record of the display material seemed a logical step.

The Kingsway exhibition was largely the conception of Gareth Dowdell, Director of the Glamorgan-Gwent Archaeological Trust. As ever, with a firm commitment to presenting the results of his organization's work to the people that matter, South Glamorgan County Council was approached for the necessary support. This was offered in no short measure, particularly in the provision of the display cases at the underpass. I should like to add my thanks to those already expressed by the Trust.

During the production of the text, and more especially during the research for illustrative material, many individuals and official bodies generously gave freely of their time. In particular, I should like to thank Tony Daly, Brenda Griffiths, Jane Hill-Kann and Tony Long of the Glamorgan-Gwent Archaeological Trust. In addition the staffs at the Departments of Archaeology and Art at the National Museum of Wales, the Welsh Industrial and Maritime Museum, the Welsh Folk Museum (St Fagans) and the Royal Commission on Ancient and Historical Monuments in Wales, have all been most helpful. The final appearance of the book has also benefited greatly from the keen interest shown by Bob Whitaker at D Brown and Sons.

Throughout the preparation of the volume I have worked closely with my friend and colleague Jim Daly of Sai Design, the designer of the original underpass exhibition. Along with Gareth Dowdell, we have, all three, talked through and sifted the material at long length. The wealth of information resulted, if anything, in the problem of knowing what we could afford to leave out, rather than what to actually include. However, I feel the completed volume is a well balanced account on the archaeology and history of this fascinating area.

The occurrence of *Heritage Year*, as well as the 10th anniversary of South Glamorgan County Council, offered an ideal dual celebration for the initial production of the book. Moreover, its publication in 1985 also marks the 10th birthday of the Glamorgan-Gwent Archaeological Trust. It is a privilege to have been associated with some of the remarkable results achieved by this body over the past decade.

David Robinson
Cardiff
Feast of St Gregory, 1985

1
Introduction:
Ruins in a Landscape

SOUTH GLAMORGAN is a new county situated within an extremely rich and historic setting. Although formed as recently as 1974, and now accommodating a population approaching 400,000, much of its present character and landscape is a direct product of man's impact over many thousands of years.

Nature's stage, the physical landscape of the county, is varied though never extreme and has attracted an unbroken chain of settlement from the dawn of history and beyond. It extends from the coastal flats situated on the eastern outskirts of Cardiff, to the gently undulating plateau known as the Vale of Glamorgan, rising to the hills of the Border Vale and the coalfield to the north. The main rivers (Ely, Taff, Thaw and Rhymney) drain this northern high ground, running through the fertile areas to the south and on into the Bristol Channel. Much of the coast is bounded with fairly steep cliffs carved by continuous wave action from the so-called Liassic and Jurassic rocks of the Vale.

Viewed from the air, it is possible to gain a reasonable impression of this natural landscape though, even here in the 'Garden of Wales' as it has been called, one is never far from the large-scale impact of man's recent developments. Indeed, superficially at least, it must be difficult to avoid the impression that sprawling modern centres such as Barry and Cardiff, huge industrial complexes such as the power stations at Aberthaw, and a multitude of road and housing developments all over the county, must surely have left little in the way of a tangible historic legacy.

A modern view of Cardiff docks from the air. Cardiff's role as perhaps the major port of South Glamorgan extends back to at least the Roman period. The advent of the Industrial Revolution brought ever increasing pressure upon the ancient harbour and in 1837 the first stone of the docks was laid. Further developments took place throughout the nineteenth century as coal exports continued to grow. By 1907 the total water area in the five principal docks had reached over 160 acres (65ha).

13

The South Glamorgan coast near Aberthaw
from the air. Aberthaw was a significant port
from the Roman period right through to the
Early Modern centuries. The vast power station
on the shoreline was originally completed in
1963, with a major second phase completed in
1975.

One of the first 'professional' archaeologists in
Wales, John Storrie. He is seen here during his
excavations at St Barruc's Chapel on Barry
Island during the summer of 1895. In his hand
he carries a steel rod shaped like a walking-stick
which he used to probe the ground for buried
remains.

14

Pausing, however, and looking deeply into the countryside, the tell-tale signs of a long and complex history begin to emerge. There are numerous monuments which bear witness to aspects of everyday life, ritual and burial, to phases of conquest and peaceful settlement and even to changing cultures and physical conditions.

A number of curious and somewhat inquisitive individuals have been aware of this legacy, and more importantly concerned with the recovery of its details, for over a century. Through their efforts and dedication these antiquaries and archaeologists have laid bare much on the way of life and character of many generations of the modern county's forefathers. One of the earliest, most colourful and energetic of these individuals was a Scotsman named John Storrie. Between 1881-93 he was the full-time curator of the then Cardiff Museum, and has been called the first professional archaeologist in Wales. Among other important discoveries, he was responsible for locating and partially excavating the Roman villas at Ely and Llantwit Major.

The seeds sown by Storrie were taken up and reaped by a distinguished line of archaeologists including John Ward, Sir Mortimer Wheeler, Sir Cyril Fox, V E Nash-Williams, W F Grimes, H N Savory and a host of others. More recently, university and State archaeological departments and units have made an enormous contribution. Thankfully, the results of all this work mean we are now in a position to present a fairly comprehensive outline on the rich and varied Heritage of South Glamorgan.

An article by John Storrie in the Western Mail *of October 26th 1899, recording Romano-British finds on Sully Moor.*

IMPORTANT FIND ON SULLY MOORS.

SKELETON, COINS, AND RINGS DISCOVERED.

BURIED FOR SIXTEEN HUNDRED YEARS.

[BY JOHN STORRIE, A.L.S.]

For many years I have been trespassing on Sully Moors. sometimes botanising, sometimes geologising, and on other like matters bent, but I little dreamt that less than six inches of clod separated me from one of the richest finds of Roman coins, &c., ever chronicled from South Wales, and I was surprised to find that last week it was found at a spot where I had often been to gather, in the sharp winds of March, the early spring mushroom (agaricus prunulus), by far the best flavoured of our native mushrooms. By the way, this spot, a field near Lavernock, and a small place on the Ely Racecourse are the only places in the district where this fungus grows, which suggests that these places might be prospected for finds. In a place exactly marked by a richer patch of grass the skeleton of a man being was found less than six inches under the surface, and within about three yards south a brass vase of small size, filled with coins

GOLD RINGS FOUND.

and some few items of jewellery, being together relics of an early time, when people banked their money in the ground to keep it safe, and safe this little hoard had been kept for 1,600 years, till an accident brought it to the light of day. It is curious to think that I, a nineteenth century man, should have eaten mushrooms nourished by the bones of that third century individual, and to speculate whether any of the qualities of the saintly or simul side of his nature have been transmitted to me through the medium of this grass. This grass, in its turn, nourished the agaric which was consumed by me, and if any of the properties of that individual is now incorporated in my frame, or have exerted any influence over me, it may explain things I have no explanation for otherwise, and may account for many objectless wanderings in out-of-the-way places to which I am subject.

To return, however, to the find of Roman coins. Last week some navvies, in the course of their work, came across the skeleton and the metal vase. A rush was made, the vase went to pieces, and each secured what he could lay hold of. One or two coins had been parted with in public-houses, and on the Friday a faint rumour got my length that old coins had been found somewhere. I spent the day in endeavouring to trace the origin of the rumour, and had given it up, as I have had to do many others, which are perpetually reaching me, and nine-tenths of which, on investigation, turn out hoaxes or mistakes, or even worse. I had, therefore, dismissed the matter from my mind and given it up, when a visitor entered my office next evening. And instantly before he had spoken, although I had never seen him or he me, I knew he knew what he knew, as the saying is, so it is needless to describe the making of a bargain between two men who want to get some advantage over the other. When dealing with plain men plain dealing is best, and at last weight for weight and "summut over" was arranged, which means that I paid weight in sovereigns for the articles, with

three sovereigns over, and silver of Victoria for both the real and the base silver or Billon coins. The shares of three of the men then passed into my possession; the fourth has taken his to Liverpool, and I am endeavouring to trace it and the missing man. My reasons for doing this is that, unless immediate action is taken when one of these finds occur, the things get scattered, and no record is kept, so that any lesson they may teach is lost to the public. Every find that is made is one less to be made, and the sources of information are becoming dried up, so it behoves one to be up and doing at every chance if these things are to be secured in their entirety for a public collection. I have notified the authorities of my possession of treasure trove in this case, and will now keep it till it is safely placed in some public collection where all such finds should go. I am engaged in cataloguing all the objects, which consists of three finger rings, four golden aureates, and 278 silver coins and a few fragments. So far as I have gone at present a golden aureas of Diocletian of about 300 A.D. is the latest coin, and from the mint state of its preservation the vase must have been buried about this date. It will be remembered that a very interesting find of Roman brass coins was made some years ago near an old Roman pottery on Coed-y-Cleron Farm, near Llanedarn. These got into private hands, and the public were never the better for the information which might have been got had they been fully examined by a competent man and publicly recorded.

SILVER COINS—REVERSES.

COPPER VASE IN WHICH THE COINS, &c., WERE FOUND.

GOLD COINS FOUND.

The Neolithic chambered tomb at Tinkinswood,
St Nicholas. The great capstone over the main
chamber is estimated to weigh some 40 tons.
When excavated it was discovered to contain the
bones of at least 50 individuals.

2
Early Prehistory: Farming and Technology

Beginnings: c 20,000-4,000 BC

The earliest man-made object yet known from Wales is a stone tool called a handaxe. This was found at Pen-y-Lan, Cardiff, and may be up to 200,000 years old, but at present this find from the dawn of mankind stands alone. Our story really begins around 20,000 years ago during the last great Ice Age. Southern Glamorgan was not fully engulfed by glaciers and there are hints that early man may have hunted for game and collected edible plants in this area.

About 8,000 BC the ice sheets began to melt and retreat northwards. The present coastline finally emerged as huge quantities of water were released into the sea. Stone tools (microliths) abandoned by food gatherers of this period, generally referred to as the Mesolithic (Middle Stone Age), are known from several points along the South Glamorgan shore including Friar's Point at Barry Island.

The Neolithic: 4,000-2,000 BC

During the ensuing Neolithic (New Stone Age) period, South Glamorgan came under the influence of the 'first farmers'. This era was to witness major advances in the control of the natural environment and the process of selective food production. The new farming culture, and all that this implied, may have arrived from the west of England by 4,000 BC.

Pottery was first introduced to south Wales at this time, and tree clearance began on a significant scale to facilitate cereal agriculture and pastoralism. A number of carefully made and often polished stone axes, used in the felling of trees, have been found at several places in South Glamorgan including Colwinston, Cowbridge and St Fagans. Other examples of finds associated with this period are well fashioned flint arrowheads, often in the shape of a leaf, which were probably used in hunting.

By far the most impressive remnants of these first agriculturalists, however, are their vast stone burial monuments known as megalithic tombs. Those at St Lythans and Tinkinswood are spectacular examples. From the bones contained in these tombs we can be sure they were built for the communal burial of the dead, but we cannot say if they were intended for single families or the chiefs of a tribal group.

The Bronze Age: c 2,000-450 BC

The tradition of multiple burial in large tombs had declined by around 2,000 BC. This appears to have been related to major cultural changes introduced to Britain as a whole, and may have resulted from an incursion of peoples from the Continent. In any case, the spread of early metal technology was taking place at this time, and seems to have been closely bound with the appearance of the so-called Beaker culture. This was named after a characteristic form of pottery drinking vessel placed in graves with the dead.

The Beaker peoples were undoubtedly metal users, but it was the transition in metal-working, from the production of a few simple

Map of major Neolithic and Bronze Age sites in South Glamorgan. The map shows the larger 'field monuments', but there are also many hundreds of sites where chance finds of flint and bronze implements have been discovered throughout the county.

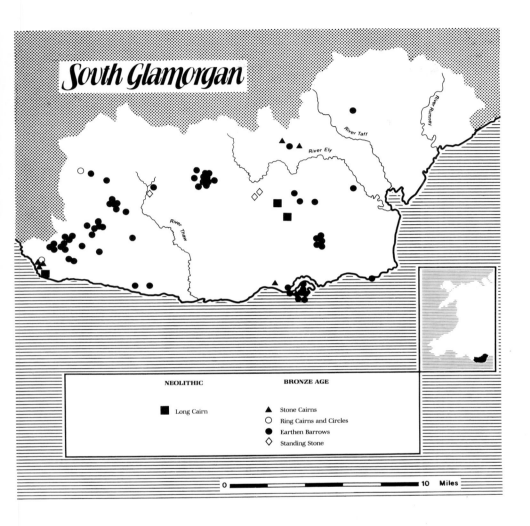

South Glamorgan

NEOLITHIC   BRONZE AGE

■ Long Cairn   ▲ Stone Cairns
                        ○ Ring Cairns and Circles
                        ● Earthen Barrows
                        ◇ Standing Stone

0 ▬▬▬▬▬▬▬▬▬▬ 10   Miles

Imaginative reconstruction of how a Neolithic stone axe may have been used. The inset shows the rare survival, found just outside South Glamorgan, of an axe still preserved in its wooden haft. Once felled, the trees would have been burnt to create clearings and provide areas for arable cultivation.

An example of the characteristic pottery vessels known as beakers. This was found by chance during the laying of a water-pipe at St Fagans around the turn of the century. It was accompanied by two burials, probably of 'beaker folk'.

A superb collection of 'barbed-and-tanged' Bronze Age arrowheads in honey-coloured and grey flint from a barrow at Breach Farm, Llanblethian. The barrow was excavated in 1937 by W F Grimes and contained a central cremation pit, together with other implements of Early to Middle Bronze Age date.

tools and ornaments in copper, to the manufacture of a wider range of artifacts made from the alloying of copper with tin, which really marks the advent of the Bronze Age.

These changes did not represent a complete break with the past. The population continued to expand and clearance for agriculture progressed, though unfortunately we are largely dependent on the survival of burial monuments for the interpretation of developments in South Glamorgan during the Beaker and Bronze Age periods.

In the Vale such tombs are largely round earthen mounds called barrows, and several early ones containing beakers are known from the south-west of Cowbridge. A number of examples have been excavated, including two recently at Welsh St Donats.

The tradition of burial within tumuli or barrows continued into the middle of the Bronze Age, though in the main cremation rather than inhumation became more common practice. Examples of this later form are known from Barry Island and Pencoedtre.

The grave goods found in many of these barrows demonstrate the technological advances made during the Bronze Age. Flint work reached new heights but was now accompanied by well fashioned tools and weapons such as daggers and spear heads cast in bronze.

By the later Bronze Age there is yet further evidence for developments in metal technology. Indeed, south-east Wales may well have had its own distinctive bronze industry specializing in the manufacture of a form of socketed axe-head.

A Bronze Age spear head from South Glamorgan. The developments which can be identified in such weapons demonstrate important technological advances at this time.

Previous Pages:

The impressive chambered long cairn of Maesyfelin, St Lythans. The tomb has never been excavated, but the main chamber comprises three large upright stones supporting a single great capstone. Such monuments are generally interpreted as 'communal' burial chambers, but their function and importance within Neolithic society may have extended well beyond this.

3
A Celtic World and the Roman Province

The Iron Age: c 450 BC-AD 75

One of the most significant events to emerge from the last one thousand years BC was the apparent division of Wales into several main tribal areas, with the south-east (including what is now South Glamorgan) eventually becoming the province of the Silures. This was accompanied by the gradual replacement of bronze by iron as the metal in most common everyday use and heralds what we now call the Iron Age.

The developments at this time may well have been related to a general migration of peoples westward in Europe as a whole. As a result, during the last 400 years before the arrival of the Roman legions, South Glamorgan became more of a part of the European world at large than ever before. On present evidence, the settlements, art style, culture and, indeed, language of the peoples concerned are seen as representing the culmination of Celtic achievements in prehistoric Europe.

The Silures of south-eastern Wales were never among the most advanced of Celtic tribes. They did not, for example, develop their own coinage or distinct pottery style. Nevertheless, they have left a rich legacy in South Glamorgan in the form of various types of walled or embanked enclosures, conventionally referred to as hillforts, or promontory forts when situated on the coast.

Examples are known from Sully Island, Porthkerry (the Bulwarks), Summerhouse

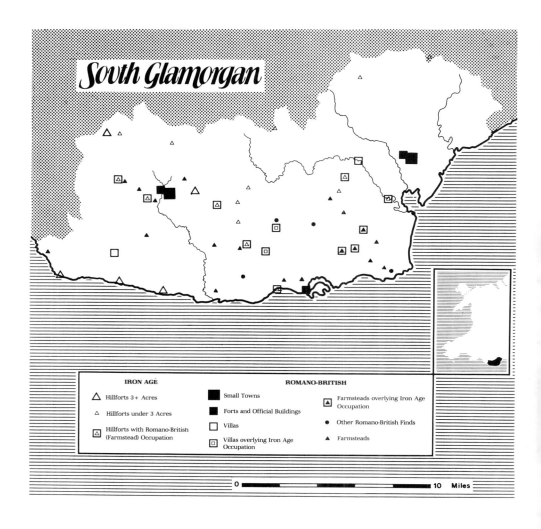

South Glamorgan

IRON AGE

△ Hillforts 3+ Acres

△ Hillforts under 3 Acres

⊡ Hillforts with Romano-British (Farmstead) Occupation

ROMANO-BRITISH

■ Small Towns

■ Forts and Official Buildings

☐ Villas

⊡ Villas overlying Iron Age Occupation

⊡ Farmsteads overlying Iron Age Occupation

● Other Romano-British Finds

▲ Farmsteads

0 ▬▬▬▬▬▬ 10 Miles

Map of major Iron Age and Romano-British sites in South Glamorgan. We now appreciate that many more farmsteads and other sites of both periods await discovery in the fields and farmlands of this area.

The hillfort of Castle Ditches, Llancarfan from the air. The defences of the fort are marked by the large oval single line of trees and enclose some 10.5 acres (4.2ha). It represents one of the largest Silurian strongholds in southern Glamorgan.

An Iron Age promontory fort at Nash Point. This aerial view shows four ramparts defending an area which originally must have been about 3.5 acres (1.4ha), but much has been lost as the cliff is eroded by wave action. A series of these forts along the South Glamorgan shore must have been ideally placed to survey Channel movements.

The excavated remains of late Iron Age round houses, Whitton Cross Roads. The site was examined by M G Jarrett between 1965-70 and found to be occupied between AD 30 and 340. These round trenches represent the bases of upright timber walls and probably date to the immediate pre-Roman conquest period.

Camp (Llantwit Major), Caer Dynnaf (Llan-blethian) and Castle Ditches (Llancarfan). The area enclosed by their often elaborate defences varies from less than an acre to over twelve acres (0.4-5.0ha). These hillforts and promontory forts are unlikely to have been purely military, and probably served as places of refuge, fortified settlements made necessary by an insecure social environment where disorder and warfare were usual. Although few sites have been excavated in south Wales, we can infer from evidence elsewhere in Britain that the defences of these forts enclosed varying numbers of round timber huts for living and other structures for grain storage.

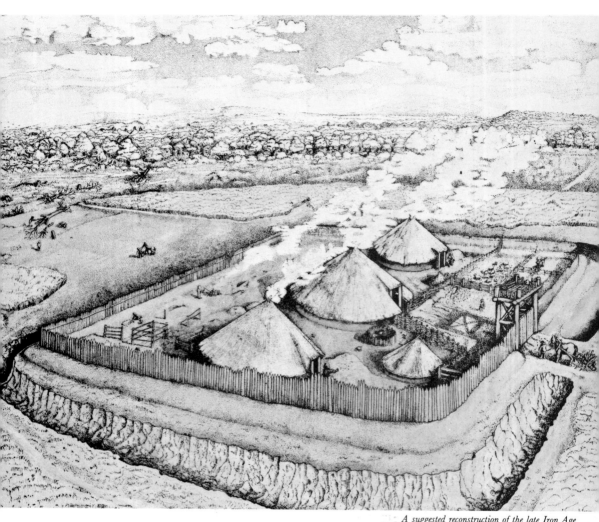

A suggested reconstruction of the late Iron Age farmstead at Whitton Cross Roads as it may have appeared around AD 55-70. This may well have been typical of the sort of domestic housing throughout the area at this time.

An imaginative reconstruction of an Iron Age smithing scene. By the closing centuries of the first millennium BC iron had replaced bronze as the predominant metal in everyday use. Smithing techniques improved as the centuries progressed.

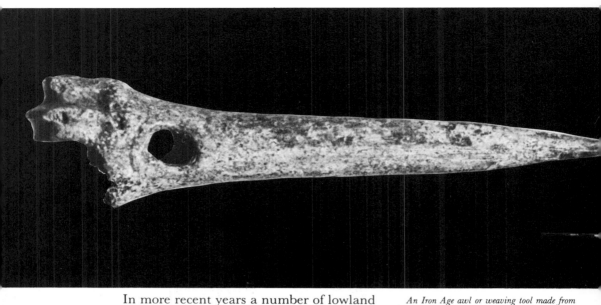

In more recent years a number of lowland late Iron Age settlements have been excavated in South Glamorgan, including sites at Biglis and Whitton. These have also been found to contain several round timber huts, but we cannot be sure if they belonged to a single extended family or a group of families working together.

It has been suggested that the hillforts and surrounding lowland farms may have been bound up with a tribal hierarchy, with the countryside divided into a network of estates. We can be sure, however, that despite the undoubted increase in the importance of metalworking, farming remained the predominant element in the economy.

An Iron Age awl or weaving tool made from animal bone. It was discovered during excavations at Biglis near Palmerstown, Barry.

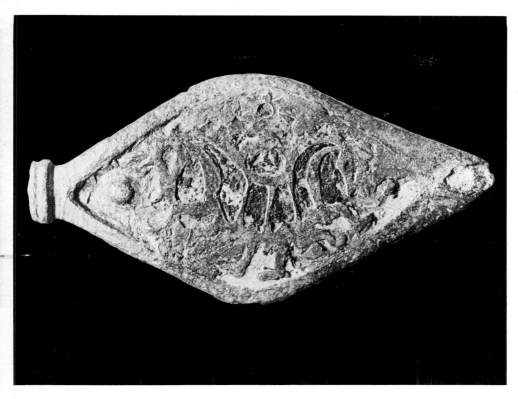

A Romano-Celtic brooch from excavations at Biglis, Barry. The well made brooch is made of bronze with enamel decoration. The drawing reveals that it clearly depicts a stylized version of a classical theme, namely the sun god (Sol) upon a chariot pulled by two horses.

Following Pages:

Roman legionary soldiers attacking a Celtic hill-fort. This imaginary scene must have been comparatively common during the early conquest years, from large sites in southern England such as Hod Hill and Maiden Castle, to the somewhat smaller forts in south-east Wales.

The Romano-British Period: c AD 75-AD 450

British prehistory was effectively brought to an end by the conquests of the Roman legions in the years following AD 43. However, despite a rapid advance across southern England, the army met with considerable opposition from the Celtic tribes of Wales, particularly the Silures in the south-east. It was not until about AD 75-80 that the present area of South Glamorgan was finally subjugated by forces of the Second Augustan Legion based at Caerleon (Gwent).

South Wales was consolidated within the new Roman province of *Britannia* by the establishment of a network of auxiliary forts including sites in South Glamorgan at Cardiff and probably Cowbridge (*Bovium*). This firm military presence was not required for very long and for the following three centuries, under the settled conditions brought about by Roman administration, the agricultural and other resources of southern Glamorgan were exploited to the full.

Over many years we have learnt a great deal about this region during the Roman period, yet the archaeologist's spade is constantly making fresh and exciting discoveries. In the countryside, for example, the height of Romanization is marked by several large and luxurious villas such as Ely, Llantwit Major and the recently discovered site at Llandough. Surrounding these villas lay a multitude of lesser farmsteads, many of which have been identified in the eastern Vale of Glamorgan including Biglis, Cadoxton, Dinas Powys Common and Llanbethery. What is more, it has recently become clear that many of these Romano-British sites directly overlie late Iron Age farmsteads and appear to demonstrate a

37

level of continuity despite the disruptive years of the conquest. This has been most clearly illustrated at Whitton Lodge in the central Vale.

The high level of agricultural activity at this time undoubtedly generated the need for market centres. In response, small towns appear to have grown up around the earlier forts at Cardiff and Cowbridge. In these centres surpluses could be sold whereas pottery and other specialist goods could be bought from craftsmen and traders.

Finds of coins, glassware, jewellery and imported and local pottery all bear witness to the level of Romanization in both the small towns and the countryside during this period.

By the late third century, however, hostile barbarian tribes from Ireland, Scotland and mainland Europe presented an ever increasing threat to the stable conditions brought by Rome. A new fort was constructed at Cardiff, bearing a close resemblance to those situated around the south-east coast of England intended to ward off the possibility of Saxon invasions. In addition, the recently discovered building at Cold Knap, Barry may present further evidence of attention to coastal protection at the time.

Despite all efforts, the growing threats, coupled with Continental difficulties, led to the final withdrawal of the Roman legions from Britain. Consequently, during the fifth century, South Glamorgan gradually took on a new aspect as the effects of Rome became eclipsed in what are still called the Dark Ages.

A section of the Roman road across the Vale of Glamorgan can be seen well preserved in the modern road alignment. Looking eastwards the A48 detours around the small town at Cowbridge, whereas the former Roman alignment is picked up in the line of hedgerows on St Hilary Down.

A selection of fine imported Roman pot' ·v known as Samian found at many sites in South Glamorgan. It was originally introduced with the Roman army, and was only gradually replaced as locally produced fine wares gained control of the market.

Following Pages:

The north gate of Cardiff Castle restored in the nineteenth century on Roman foundations, gives an excellent impression of the defences of a later Roman fort. The gate and defences represent what was probably a fourth fort at Cardiff, constructed during the later third century in response to the ever increasing threat of barbarian invasion.

4
The Medieval Period: Darkness and Enlightenment

The Dark Ages: c AD 450-AD 1100

A late ninth century Early Christian Monument from Llantwit Major known as the Houelt *stone. It is likely to commemorate Hywel ap Rhys, king of Glywysing who died in AD 886.*

An eighth century burial cut into the demolition deposits of an earlier Romano-British villa at Llandough. The proximity of the parish church dedicated to St Dochdwy suggests early Christian activity in the area.

Unfortunately, our knowledge of the political and economic history of Wales as a whole during the centuries following the collapse of Roman rule is particularly sparse. Few reliable documentary sources survive and, hitherto, archaeological evidence has not proved especially enlightening.

We can, however, be sure that following its introduction to later Roman Britain, Christianity became the overwhelming religious belief in early medieval Wales. Indeed, there are suggestions that the final inhabitants of the large villa at Llantwit Major were Christians.

Even so, although there is reasonable documentary evidence from the later part of this period to attest to important 'monastic' foundations in South Glamorgan at Llantwit Major, Llancarfan and Llandough it is extremely difficult to say when, or how far back, they were actually founded. There is even greater difficulty in trying to assess what such sites mean in terms of physical evidence on the ground.

A clearer indication of Christian activity is perhaps the collection of tombstones and crosses collectively known as early Christian monuments. Over 400 are recorded from Wales, with dates ranging from the fifth to the eleventh centuries, and include a number from South Glamorgan. Once again, in this area, they are somewhat late and belong to the tenth and eleventh centuries.

43

Further important information on Christianity has been recovered from excavations at Llandough. A number of skeletons was recovered from archaeological levels overlying a Roman-British villa, and have been shown by radio-carbon dating to belong to the eighth century. Thus, there are strong hints of continuity between the former villa and the important Christian monastery known to have existed in the vicinity.

On the domestic side, until recently the only recorded site of the period was discovered at Dinas Powys. When excavated, a few small buildings were found to lie within simple defences and were apparently occupied between the fifth and seventh centuries. From the quality of finds recovered, including pottery imported from the Mediterranean, the site has been interpreted as the court (*llys*) of a petty lord or chieftain.

A second domestic site of the period is now known from Cold Knap, Barry, where a small round-cornered stone building, radio-carbon dated to the turn of the ninth century, was found to overlie an earlier Roman structure.

Finally, although there are indications of Viking activity around the South Glamorgan coast, particularly the evidence of place-names, we have yet to identify any surviving archaeological sites of such a Norse origin.

Map of major Dark Age and Medieval sites in South Glamorgan. In addition to the sites illustrated, virtually every parish church and nucleated village originated during these centuries.

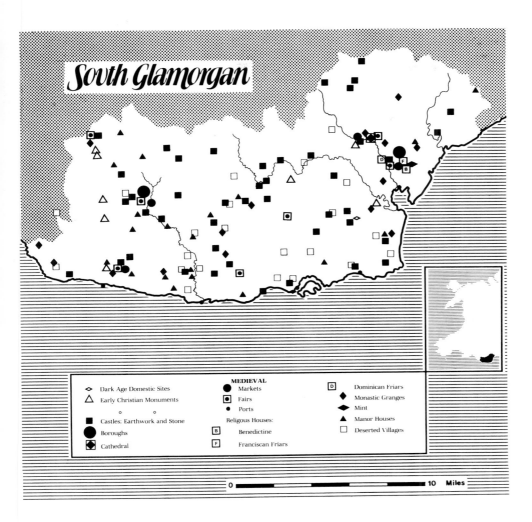

South Glamorgan

MEDIEVAL

⬦ Dark Age Domestic Sites	● Markets	D Dominican Friars
△ Early Christian Monuments	⊡ Fairs	◆ Monastic Granges
○　　　○	● Ports	◆ Mint
■ Castles: Earthwork and Stone	Religous Houses:	▲ Manor Houses
● Boroughs	B Benedictine	☐ Deserted Villages
⬤ Cathedral	F Franciscan Friars	

0 ▬▬▬▬▬▬▬▬ 10 Miles

45

The Middle Ages: c AD 1100-AD 1500

In the closing years of the eleventh century, South Glamorgan was brought once more into the mainstream of English political and cultural events. The arrival of the Normans, under Robert Fitzhamon, put an end to the independence of this part of Wales.

The rich and fertile land of South Glamorgan was one of the first areas to be conquered, just as it had been in Roman times. As a result, the former Welsh kingdom of Morgannwg was henceforward to become the medieval marcher lordship of Glamorgan. The lordship, and its controlling lord, became extremely powerful over the Middle Ages, and many vestiges of the period survive in the present landscape.

To begin with, Glamorgan is rightly called a land of castles, and most were established at this time as footholds for the Norman advance and in order to consolidate territorial gain. During the conquest years they tended to be built of earth and timber, as in the case of Fitzhamon's own motte at Cardiff. Others had almost circular earthen bank and ditch defences, which we now know as 'ringworks'. One of these has recently been comprehensively excavated at Rumney on the outskirts of Cardiff. In the later Middle Ages many of these castles were refortified in stone and, once again, the so-called shell keep on top of the motte at Cardiff is a good example. There are, however, many fine instances of later stone castles throughout South Glamorgan including Barry, Dinas Powys, Fonmon and St Donats.

A further development under the Normans was the reorganization of the church, bringing it more in line with southern England and the Continent. A new diocese was established in south-east Wales, with its centre and

Excavated remains of a Dark Age round-cornered building at Glan-y-Mor, Barry. Only a single course of stone survives, but the structure was radio-carbon dated to the turn of the ninth century. The building was constructed upon the demolition deposits of a unique Roman site. The reconstruction gives some impression of how it may have looked.

The Norman motte at Cardiff Castle
surmounted by a later stone shell-keep. The
motte was originally constructed by the first lord
of Glamorgan, Robert Fitzhamon, soon after
1081. It grew to become the centre for
administration throughout the lordship. During
the nineteenth century the castle as a whole was
greatly modified and added to by the third
marquess of Bute.

*A carefully scaled reconstruction of the late
thirteenth century castle at Barry. From the
drawing of the castle itself, the gateway,
probably constructed by the de Barri family as
lords of the manor, is seen to be the best
surviving feature. The superb model is in the
garden of a local archaeologist.*

cathedral based at Llandaff. In addition, most of the parish churches of South Glamorgan were built in stone for the first time during the medieval centuries, and many fine examples such as Llanblethian, Llancarfan, Llantwit Major, St Athan and St Hilary survive to this day. Finally, monastic life, again based on Anglo-Norman lines, was to have a significant impact on South Glamorgan. A Benedictine monastery and two friaries were founded in Cardiff, whereas other religious houses from outside the area created the nucleus of outlying estates or granges at places such as Llantwit Major and Marcross.

The medieval period also saw the introduction of 'urban' or town life to southern Wales. Chartered boroughs were a source of revenue to Norman and later lords and were, therefore, fostered throughout the marcher lordship, with good examples at Cardiff and Cowbridge. Llantwit Major also lays some claim to 'urban' status at this time, though it never appears to have been granted a formal borough charter.

Many of the nucleated villages, so familiar in the modern county of South Glamorgan, probably owe their origin to Anglo-Norman developments. Before this time the rural settlement pattern is likely to have been somewhat dispersed, but the new lords saw the economic advantages of nucleation. Not all of them have survived intact to the present day, since there is evidence of shrinkage and even desertion at sites such as Llancadle and Cosmeston. Others, though much altered, retain something of the character of the Middle Ages in their overall topography.

In many of these villages the manor house replaced the castle as the centre of control and authority and a number of such sites are known

In the very early twelfth century Llandaff was chosen as the centre of a new ecclesiastical diocese, arranged along Anglo-Norman lines. In 1120 work began on the construction of a cathedral church. Further additions, including aisles, the Lady Chapel and the Chapter House, were made in the thirteenth century. By the eighteenth century the cathedral had fallen into sad neglect. The nave had become a ruin with the roof open to the sky. The medieval structure was heavily restored during the nineteenth century, and again after bomb damage in World War Two. The Jasper Tower, seen here, is essentially fifteenth century, whereas the Prichard Spire was a nineteenth century addition.

from the county. In some cases they were surrounded by a moat as at Llysworney and Highlight.

The origin of almost all the parish churches of South Glamorgan can be traced to the early Middle Ages, particularly in the villages of the Vale. This example, in a picturesque setting at Llancarfan, became one of the largest. This view from the south-west shows the thirteenth century south aisle and fourteenth century tower. The nave and chancel lie behind the aisle.

A wine-jug from the Saintonge, north of Bordeaux (south-western France), many of which were imported in the medieval period and are found on numerous castle and manorial sites in South Glamorgan.

54

A suggested reconstruction of the moated manorial site at Highlight, Barry, as it may have appeared in the fourteenth century. Almost twenty such sites are now known from southern Glamorgan, but Highlight is the only excavated example. The site was almost certainly the centre of the sub-manor of the de Someri lordship of Dinas Powys. Occupation was discovered to range between the late twelfth and the fifteenth centuries.

Earthworks of a monastic grange at Marcross seen from the air. This was the centre of an important agricultural estate belonging to the Cistercian abbey of Neath (West Glamorgan). To the right is the B4265 Bridgend to Llantwit Major road. Beneath the turf lie the hidden remains of barns, stock pens and a variety of other buildings. Further extensive grange remains can be found in South Glamorgan, notably at Monknash. The drawing suggests a reconstruction of the immense medieval barn at the Monknash site.

55

56

5
The Early Modern Age: Reorientation and Rebuilding

c AD 1500-AD 1750

The early post-medieval centuries have been called quite correctly a period of reorientation, both in the town and in the countryside. This is certainly true of southern Wales where there were very important changes in the political and ecclesiastical arrangements under which people lived.

One of the most important events was the establishment of the *shire* of Glamorgan which emerged through the Acts of Union, under Henry VIII, between 1536-43. The new shire was to be administered through the offices of sheriff, deputy lieutenant and justice of the peace and survived essentially as founded until the local government reorganization of 1974. Under the Acts, the former medieval boroughs of Cardiff and Cowbridge were now given representation in Parliament.

This period also witnessed the Reformation and the Dissolution of the Monasteries, both with important and far reaching effects on the church and church lands. Finally, under the growing influence of changes in the economy and landholding, new and significant patterns began to emerge in the rural landscape.

Some historians have observed the extent to which many of these changes reflect the opportunities taken by a rising gentry class, taking advantage of the reforms in both church and state. But within the heritage of the modern county, there is also evidence of pros-

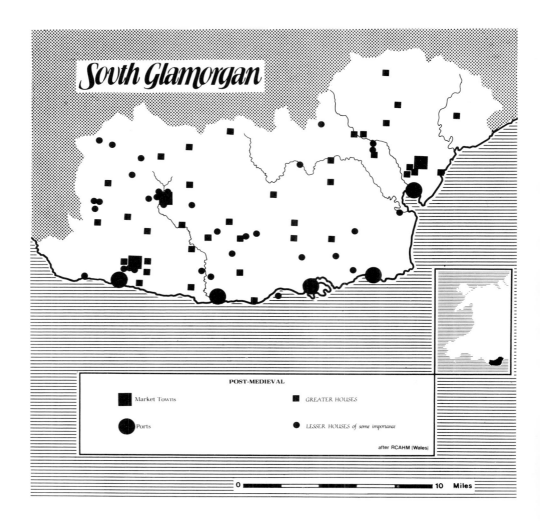

South Glamorgan

POST-MEDIEVAL

■ Market Towns

● Ports

■ GREATER HOUSES

● LESSER HOUSES of some importance

after RCAHM [Wales]

0 ▬▬▬▬▬▬▬▬▬▬ 10 Miles

Previous Pages:

Detail from a panoramic view of Cardiff from the west, as seen by Samuel and Nathaniel Buck in the 1740s. Such prints by the Buck brothers are milestones in the recording of topographic detail, and provide us with tremendous insight into the nature of historic sites at this period.

Map of the principal buildings and sites of the Early Modern centuries in South Glamorgan. In addition to houses, which are the major feature of this map, it is important to bear in mind that many medieval structures, for example, continued in use and were modified at this time. Parish churches and urban or municipal buildings are cases in point.

perous 'yeomen' farmers, as well as adventurers and entrepreneurs of this period.

To begin with, although a number of the medieval boroughs of the marcher lordship of Glamorgan had declined, Cardiff and Cowbridge continued to prosper. Llantwit Major also retained an urban rank at this time, and in all three there is much evidence of rebuilding. The Great House in Cowbridge, Ty Mawr, the Swan and White Hart inns and the Town Hall in Llantwit Major are all good examples. Whereas for Cardiff, we can get a very good impression of the culmination of events in the period in studying the panoramic view of the town produced by the Buck brothers in the 1740s.

In the countryside there is a wealth of detail on what has been called the *Great Rebuilding*. There are, for example, many large or greater houses which belonged to the gentry classes. Some such as Beaupre and St Donats represent a remodelling of earlier castles. Others like Flemingston Court, Llanmihangel Place, Llansannor Court and Rhiwperra were constructions in new and interesting styles.

Less grand, but also of great interest, are the large numbers of well-built yeomen farmhouses of these early post-medieval centuries. These can be seen in villages or standing in isolation throughout South Glamorgan. They were all built in stone, often with thatched roofs and examples include the Blue Anchor Inn (Aberthaw), To Hesg (Llantwit Major), Breach (Llanblethian), together with many others.

Changes in the church meant the former monasteries and the centres of their estates fell into gradual decay. In the parishes, the Reformation resulted in the confiscation of many church goods. Later still, in the seventeenth

The magnificent storeyed porch enriched with classical detail, built in 1600 at Old Beaupre. This feature is the glory of the once medieval castle, modified and added to in the sixteenth century largely by Sir Rice Mansel and Sir Richard Basset. It represents one of the greater houses of the landed gentry of this period.

Castle Farm, now known as Flemingston Court, lying in the small village of Flemingston. It was built by a minor gentry family during the early sixteenth century. It is a classic example of a storeyed construction of the medieval hall-house tradition, with a lateral fireplace and chimney serving the great hall. A cross-passage, marked by the pointed doorway, divides the hall from the service rooms to the right.

century, the effects of the Commonwealth led to the destruction of much of the medieval imagery in churches.

The early modern period also saw the enclosure of many of the former 'open fields'. The medieval strips were gradually amalgamated to form smaller enclosed fields, still characteristic of South Glamorgan today. A series of maps produced by Evans Mouse in the 1620s shows how this had taken place on the Fonmon estates by this time. One, for example, shows the manor of Barry in 1622.

Farming continued to be the most important element in the economy, and the existence of large barns for the threshing of grain demonstrates the importance of home grown corn throughout and beyond these centuries.

In contrast to these general patterns, there is always the unique and unexpected in South Glamorgan. There is no finer example than Marsh House at East Aberthaw. Here, in the mid 1630s, a local entrepreneur named Thomas Spencer built what amounted to almost the last castle in Wales. He constructed for himself a fortified compound used for the storage of illegally imported tobacco and probably other valuable cargoes. These were released onto the market when prices were highest.

Thus, the county is rich in evidence for significant changes in direction accompanied by extensive new building programmes over this period.

*The Blue Anchor Inn at East Aberthaw.
Although it is now a public house, it was
originally a farmhouse belonging to the early
post-medieval centuries. The doorway marks the
former entry to the kitchen, with the hall and
inner rooms to the left and a later bakehouse
addition to the right. Many original features are
still to be seen within the interior.*

A former farmhouse at Breach, Llanblethian. It represents a typical Vale house of the mid seventeenth century.

The former 'Town Hall' at Llantwit Major, which dates to the seventeenth century. Similar examples are known to have existed in St Mary's Street at Cardiff and the High Street in Cowbridge.

Following Page:

Detail from a late eighteenth century view of St Mary's Street, Cardiff by Thomas Rowlandson. At the time, it seems that many of the town's buildings were still half-timbered. The medieval town hall lies in the centre of the street, and altogether this creates an excellent impression of the character of the age.

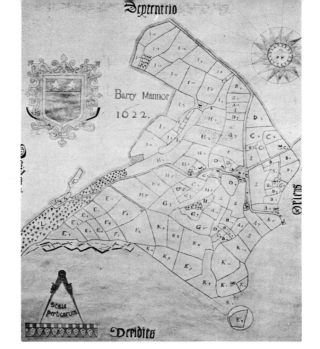

The manor of Barry as surveyed by Evans Mouse in 1622. This map shows that enclosure had already taken place in this area. The land was divided amongst some fourteen copyholders, with nine farmsteads within the area.

The fortified tobacco warehouse known as Marsh House, East Aberthaw, built about 1636. It was constructed by Thomas Spencer and virtually amounts to the last castle built in South Glamorgan. From the plan we can see that apart from a house and storerooms, a large compound is enclosed by walls pierced at intervals by musket loops. It was used to protect illegal imports of tobacco and other goods. Unfortunately the site has now been unavoidably lost through development.

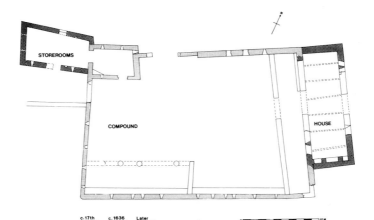

STOREROOMS

COMPOUND

HOUSE

c.17th   c.1636   Later

6
The Industrial Era: Coal, Steel, Sail and Steam

c AD 1750-AD 1914

Despite the rural charm and tranquillity encountered in rural South Glamorgan even today, few areas were left untouched by the dramatic effects of the Industrial Revolution, chiefly between 1750 and the Great War of 1914-18.

This is brought out quite poignantly in the recorded levels of the population. Even in the Vale of Glamorgan, for example, numbers rose from around 7,000 in 1750 to about 11,500 in 1820, but it was in the 'new' industrial towns that figures expanded most rapidly. This is seen at its clearest in what had been the small market town of Cardiff where, in 1801, there were just under 2,000 people. By 1861 this figure had risen to almost 42,000 and by 1901 it had reached an astonishing total of over 164,000. As we shall see, there were similar patterns elsewhere.

Having said this, it is important to be aware that farming continued to play a significant role in the economy. Although mechanization was not introduced on a massive scale, farms did tend to grow larger through amalgamation. Various farm buildings of the period have survived and, at Hayes Farm near Sully, for example, a windmill dating to around 1813 has been preserved as part of the rural heritage of the industrial age.

The seeds of the major developments in South Glamorgan, however, were sown further north in the coalfield around Merthyr Tydfil. In the late eighteenth century iron produced in

South Glamorgan

INDUSTRIAL

Railway Index

○ Ports and Docks

■ Market Towns

◡ Industrial Centres

V of G Vale of Glamorgan Railway
G W R Great Western Railway
T V R Taff Vale Railway
B R Barry Railway
R R Rhymney Railway
C R Cardiff Railway

Canal & Railways c.1905

╱ Canal

✦ Railways

0 ▬▬▬▬▬▬ 10 Miles

Previous Pages:

The Industrial Revolution did not mean a complete break with the rural past, particularly in the Vale of Glamorgan. This is a typical ploughing scene near the close of the industrial age.

Map of major features of the industrial age in South Glamorgan. In the main this demonstrates the growth of ports and the advent of the railways.

this area was exported through the comparatively small port of Cardiff. Coal was also exported at the time, but transportation from north to south presented great difficulties. The 'revolution' began in 1794 with the opening of the Glamorganshire Canal, thereby linking Cardiff with the northern part of the county, and enabling a vastly increased tonnage to reach the port.

During the nineteenth century, coal mining gradually replaced iron smelting as the dominant industrial activity in the eastern valleys of the old county. By the middle of the century, Cardiff had become the greatest coal-exporting port in the world. The town, which on a map of 1828 was still very much confined to its medieval walled core, began to expand rapidly with new industrial housing spreading over former fields and rural villages such as Canton and Roath. A map of the town centre prepared in 1851 shows how swiftly developments had taken place there.

The mid eighteenth century was still the heyday of the sailing ship, and the Bute West Dock, which had opened in 1839, constantly appeared as a forest of masts. There was little doubt that, if the demand for coal was to continue to rise, then the congestion must somehow be relieved.

Further strain was placed on the port with the opening of the Taff Vale Railway between Cardiff and Abercynon in 1840, and the link to Merthyr Tydfil in the following year. Yet larger quantities of coal could now reach the coast. As for the railways, this was merely the beginning of their impact on the industrial age.

In 1865 a new dock was opened at Penarth, which helped remove the mounting congestion at Cardiff for some time. The dock, together with its attendant rail links, trans-

Following Pages:

The eighteen-pier railway viaduct spanning the valley of the small Whitelands Brook in Porthkerry Park. When constructed it linked the new port of Barry with the coalfields of northern Glamorgan. It remains an extremely impressive monument to the railway age.

71

Hayes Farm Windmill, near Sully. It was
built about 1813 and was originally wind-
powered with a revolving cap. By the end of the
nineteenth century, however, it had been
converted to a horse driven system, and later
still to petrol engine propulsion. The mill has
been preserved with its wooden gears and three
millstones intact.

A stretch of the Glamorganshire Canal, completed in 1794. It was a tremendous engineering achievement for its day, and linked the iron town of Merthyr Tydfil with the port at Cardiff. In all, it ran through a landfall of 468 feet (143m) and included some 40 locks. On reaching Cardiff it ran along the eastern outskirts of the town in line with the former castle moat and town ditch.

Congested shipping in Bute Dock, Cardiff, 1866 appears as a forest of masts. The success of the docks during the nineteenth century led to an astonishing rise in the population of the town.

formed the small seaside resort of just over 1,400 people in 1861, to a considerable urban centre of almost 13,000 souls in 1891.

Still the demand for Welsh steam coal rose, and alternatives had to be found if the South Glamorgan coast was to cope with export. In 1884 the Barry Dock and Railway Company was formed and a site chosen for a new dock between Barry Island and the mainland. It was opened in 1889 with such success that a further dock was soon under construction and came into use in 1898. Both docks were linked to the coalfields by almost 70 miles of track belonging to the Barry Railway and its subsidiary, the Vale of Glamorgan Railway. Once again the story is told in the population figures which mushroomed from just 500 in 1881 to an incredible 39,000 in 1921.

The development and expansion of the railways is a history in itself. From the beginnings in the 1840s, the second half of the nineteenth century was a period of intense competition between railway companies grabbing as much as they could from the profitable coal trade. Some have already been mentioned, but others such as the Cardiff, Rhymney and South Wales Railways all played their part. Although much has disappeared, there are imposing relics such as the superb Porthkerry viaduct still surviving in the South Glamorgan landscape. Many people, of course, lament the passing of the paddle and steam ship. How the three large ports must have resounded to the noise of both in the late nineteenth century.

The industrial era brought its problems as well as its advantages, particularly the difficulties of housing such a rapidly expanding population. Each year more of the streets which were hurriedly constructed at this time are now bulldozed to make way for modern develop-

The docks at Barry were begun in 1884 in response to increasing pressure upon the facilities at Cardiff and Penarth. The first dock was opened in 1889 and soon led to a mushrooming population and new town. This view, around the turn of the century, shows a paddle steamer in the foreground, with the large offices of the Barry Railway Company to the rear.

Industrial housing of the nineteenth century typified by a view of Jones Court, Cardiff. Such housing was constructed rapidly to accommodate the booming population of the new 'industrial towns'.

ments. It becomes ever more difficult for us to imagine the squalor suffered by so many families in the name of progress. Early photographs, however, do much to bring scenes from this 'frontier' period to life.

In contrast, this was also an age of intense public building with hospitals, libraries, theatres and administrative buildings all being constructed in the towns. What is more, large private building programmes were undertaken by those families and individuals with wealth gained in the coal and shipping trades. Cardiff Castle, for example, was restored as a romantic vision of the Middle Ages between 1868-90 by the third marquess of Bute. The architect he employed, William Burges, went on to produce yet finer glories at Castell Coch. In the countryside the new wealth was displayed in such grandiose structures as Dyffryn House, rebuilt by the shipowner John Cory in 1893.

One final feature of this period which is worthy of some note is the rise of the nonconformist church, particularly the Baptists, the Welsh Wesleyan Methodists and the Calvinistic Methodists. Although the origins go back to the seventeenth century, the groups were few in number until the turn of the eighteenth century. The beliefs, however, took firm root and chapels were established in all the larger villages of South Glamorgan. Many of these chapels, chiefly built in the period 1800-50, still survive in the county, though a number have been converted to alternate uses.

A scene during the riot on the corner of Bute Street and Custom House Street, Cardiff in 1892.

A former Methodist chapel at Llancarfan now converted to a modern house. Many more nonconformist chapels survive in their original state throughout the country.

An aerial view of the large Iron Age hillfort at Caerau, Ely. The fort covers an area of some 12.6 acres (5.1ha) and is to become the focus of the County's new Heritage Park.

7
Conservation: Guarding Your Heritage

Throughout this book stress is laid upon a very long period of human occupation and activity, a period which has given rise to a rich and varied heritage which can be seen in all parts of modern South Glamorgan. The story does not, however, end in 1914, not for that matter in 1984. Developments are far from static, since demands for new road and housing schemes, shopping and recreational facilities, to name just a few, appear to increase almost every year. Indeed, it is probably true to say that the rate of change is now faster than ever before. With this in mind, questions of conservation and the steps taken to guard our valuable heritage assume considerable importance.

Despite the rapid pace of change, not just in South Glamorgan but in Britain as a whole, one of the most heartening aspects of the last two decades has been a growing concern for our environment. National and local authorities, as well as individuals, are now fully aware that further development is inevitable, but they also appreciate the need to combine it with thought and care for the environment. Such concern not only includes the natural landscapes of field, river, coast or woodland, but also extends to our vulnerable historic past. In South Glamorgan we are extremely fortunate to have a local authority which is deeply concerned with such matters.

There are many projects and schemes which could be cited as examples of such conservation, but it is as well to begin with one combining both elements of the natural and the historic environment. In 1973 the *Glamorgan*

Heritage Coast was established to protect and encourage people to enjoy the beauty of one of the finest stretches of coastline in Britain. It extends from Ogmore in the west, almost to Aberthaw in the east, with a considerable section lying in the new county of South Glamorgan. Since its foundation in 1974, the County Council has given full support to this project, thereby fostering interest and ensuring protection for three Iron Age promontory forts at Nash Point, Castle Ditches (Llantwit Major) and Summerhouse Point. A Heritage Centre has now been established and, although situated outside the county at Dunraven, it has much information on all aspects of this coastline.

As a result of the Civic Amenities Act of 1967, a number of so-called 'Conservation Areas' have been designated in South Glamorgan and have again been supported by the new Council. In particular they cover the two historic towns of Cowbridge and Llantwit Major, but also extend to larger villages. Under the terms of the Act attempts have been made to protect and enhance the character of whole areas rather than individual sites or structures.

In this context, a new project to be undertaken by the County Council at Caerau on the outskirts of Cardiff is a very exciting prospect. At the centre of the project is the large Iron Age hillfort of Caerau itself, now bounded by the southern access road to the city. Within this hillfort lies what is now the sad ruin of a medieval church. Unfortunately, this has fallen into neglect and decay, and more recently has proved a target for vandalism. However, the entire complex is now to become a Heritage Park with an interpretive centre and other facilities. Situated as it is, so close to Cardiff, it will no doubt prove a popular attraction.

A stretch of the Glamorgan Heritage Coast from the air. This view is centred upon the Iron Age promontory fort of Summerhouse Point. It is possible to walk along considerable lengths of this scenic coast towards the western shore of the county.

The island of Flat Holm from the air. It forms
the focus of a County conservation scheme and
has many interesting historic features. The
island lighthouse dates back to 1738, and in
1860 the island was fortified with four batteries
of guns within the rocks as part of a defence
scheme for the Channel ports.

The south gate into the former medieval borough of Cowbridge. There were originally four gates into the town which, together with the walls, were constructed around the close of the thirteenth century. Only the south gate (Porth-y-Felin) survives, and has recently been carefully restored by the County Council.

Similar interpretive and conservation programmes have been underway at the county's
two very attractive offshore islands. The one at
Sully, again with an Iron Age promontory fort,
and the other at Flat Holm which has a full and
fascinating history.

Turning to individual sites and buildings,
the County Council has done much to promote
public awareness and interest through the production of its *County Treasures Survey*. This series
of booklets, which cover individual or groups of
parishes, provide brief details on a wide variety
of architectural, archaeological and historic
features of all periods. They point out that the
deterioration or destruction of any such features would represent a serious loss to our
heritage.

Related to such interests, the County ad-
ministers an Historic Buildings Fund. Once
again it reflects concern for the rich stock of
structures of considerable architectural importance. The Fund provides grant aid for repair
and maintenance, where otherwise cheap or
poor workmanship would result in an irreplace-
able loss to the area's heritage. Buildings which
have so far benefited from the scheme include
Cogan Hall Farm at Sully and the 'Ancient
Druid' in Eastgate at Cowbridge.

A further aspect to conservation is the
conversion or new uses found for some of the
large country houses situated throughout the
county. Cefn Mably, for example, has become
a hospital, whereas the once medieval castle at
St Donats is now an international sixth form
college. Dyffryn House, on the other hand, is a
centre for day and residential educational
courses, and its fine gardens are open to the
public.

Finally, the County Council has frequently shown the good will and aptitude to

The east front of the impressive Elizabethan mansion at St Fagans. Constructed upon the site of a medieval castle, this multi-gabled appearance is typical in houses of the Renaissance period. The castle and grounds today form the focus of the Welsh Folk Museum, housing a large collection on the material culture of Wales.

Previous Pages:

Dyffryn House, St Nicholas, built for the Cardiff shipowner John Cory in 1893. It is now an educational centre run by the County, with superb gardens displayed to the general public.

cope with emergencies. Recently the medieval south gate at Cowbridge, for example, was saved from extensive decay through a comprehensive programme of restoration work. Perhaps an even greater achievement, however, was the part played by the Council in the salvation of the unique Roman building unearthed at Cold Knap, Barry in 1980. This virtually unexpected find would have been bulldozed away and the site occupied by a modern housing development had the Council not stepped forward with the necessary funding. Since that time the Council has gone on to play a major role in the conservation and landscaping of the site, all of which means that a fascinating Roman structure will now be on permanent display to the general public.

    With so much general concern there would appear to be great hopes for the future of our rich heritage in South Glamorgan.

A mason at work on reconsolidation at the Roman building, Cold Knap, Barry in 1981. Thanks to the work of the County Council (together with the Vale of Glamorgan Borough Council and the Welsh Office), the site was saved from the clutches of development and is now on permanent display to the public.

*The marvellous setting of the extensive Roman
building at Glan-y-Mor, Cold Knap in Barry.*

8
Rescue Archaeology: Cardiff and the East

Despite talk of cut-backs and the economic recession which has gripped Britain over the past few years, south-east Wales remains a rapidly expanding region. The urban centres of Barry and Cardiff are among the largest in the Principality which, together with the overall population density, continues to place great pressure on the heritage of South Glamorgan. Despite considerable good will on the part of the local authority, as well as other concerned bodies and individuals, it is almost inevitable that year by year further archaeological and historical sites are destroyed to make way for modern developments.

By the mid 1970s it had become increasingly self-evident to those responsible for the distribution of archaeological funds in Wales, that the existing system of scattered support for various projects was totally inefficient for the needs of the time. There finally emerged an appreciation of the true level of *Rescue* work that ought to be undertaken in advance of total destruction. With development threats increasing each year, if archaeological sites were to be examined in sufficient numbers, and on a realistic time-scale, then a revised system of organization was desperately required. As a result, between 1974-75 four regional archaeological Trusts, with specific responsibility for rescue excavations, were established in the four corners of Wales.

In the south-east, including the area of South Glamorgan, the Glamorgan-Gwent Archaeological Trust was set up in the closing months of 1975. It was originally based at

An aerial view of the excavations at the late Bronze Age hill-slope fort at Coed-y-Cymdda, Wenvoe. The site shows up as a clearance within the trees, and was excavated in advance of total loss as the limestone quarry gradually encroached upon the site.

The east gate into the fort at Coed-y-Cymdda is marked by terminals within the rock cut ditch. The evidence suggests that antelope or deer horns were used as picks to dig out this ditch from solid limestone rock. The resulting spoil was then used to create an internal bank.

Cardiff, though soon moved to Swansea, and has operated from there very successfully ever since. In the years which have followed, demands upon the Trust and its resources have never ceased.

South Glamorgan has been particularly well served, largely due to the pace of development, and numerous excavations have been undertaken on sites of periods ranging from the prehistoric to the industrial. The results have added much to our knowledge of past developments and our historic legacy within the county.

Let us begin with several projects centred around the capital city, in the eastern part of the county. The first at Coed-y-Cymdda, a hillfort which may have had its origins in the late Bronze Age. The second at Llandough, where the details of a peviously unrecorded Romano-British villa were salvaged from the jaws of the bulldozer. Thirdly, at Rumney where the secrets of an early medieval timber castle have recently been uncovered.

The work at Coed-y-Cmdda, near Wenvoe, was on the site of a comparatively small hillfort, or in this case 'hill slope' enclosure, with evidence of several main periods of occupation. Excavations were undertaken in advance of the total destruction of the site through limestone quarrying. They began in July 1978 and continued, almost uninterrupted, until February 1980.

The site appears to have been first cleared in the late Neolithic or early Bronze Age, and various tools of this period have been recovered. However, it was probably not until the Iron Age that the enclosure was created by the cutting of a ditch in the solid limestone bedrock. There is evidence that antelope horns were used as picks to dig out this ditch, and the spoil used to create an internal bank. A large entrance was located on the northern side with a smaller one to the east. Unfortunately, although a number of flint tools and pottery finds were recovered from within the enclosure, traces of structures proved extremely difficult to locate.

The site is now one of the most fully excavated of its type in southern Wales.

At Llandough, on the southern outskirts of Cardiff, the Trust undertook emergency excavations over an eight week period in the early Summer of 1979. Important details on a substantial Romano-British villa were recovered, as well as evidence for Dark Age activity and the use of the site as a monastic grange in the Middle Ages.

Indeed, the site was originally occupied by a late Iron Age farmstead, with a defensive ditch and round timber huts. Following a short period of abandonment, the Romano-British villa was constructed in stone about AD 120-30. In the early third century additions and alterations were undertaken, and an elaborate bath complex was constructed. The villa was probably the centre of a large estate and its buildings well reflect the Romanized tastes of its owner.

By the middle of the fourth century the site had fallen out of use and it is difficult to assess precisely what occurred in the post-Roman centuries. We do, however, know from a series of radio-carbon dates that the site was apparently used as a burial ground during at least a part of the Dark Ages. Moreover, it is tempting to link these burials with somewhat later documentary evidence for an Early Christian monastic establishment somewhere in the vicinity, possibly located on or near the site of the parish church.

A probable Neolithic leaf shaped arrowhead found during the excavations at Coed-y-Cymdda.

An overall view of the excavated Romano-British villa at Llandough. The villa was occupied from the early second to the mid fourth centuries and was constructed in two main phases. This view from the north-west shows the footings of several rooms, with the once elaborate early third century bath block to the rear.

98

A detailed view of the cold plunge bath within the early third century bath complex at the Llandough villa. When built this was probably lined and decorated with painted plaster.

These iron collars, spaced at regular intervals, were used to connect wooden pipes which supplied the water to the Llandough villa. Although the wood had long since disappeared, the collars remained intact and were discovered during excavation.

The 'head' and 'tail' of a silver penny of Edward I found as part of a hoard during the excavations at Rumney Castle. The hoard was discovered below the charred remains of the castle's hall, and provided important evidence on the date of the fire and the final demise of the Castle itself.

A 'race against time'. Soon after the excavations at Llandough were completed mechanical excavators move in to level the ground and make way for a modern housing development.

It would seem from the archaeological evidence that at least a part of the villa was still standing in the thirteenth and fourteenth centuries when a grange of Tewkesbury Abbey was established at Llandough. The remains of a large barn and a dovecot associated with this grange were discovered during the excavation, and it was clear that in some cases Roman foundations had been utilized for the later medieval superstructures.

The whole complex at Llandough was an extremely exciting find since it has added much new information to our understanding of several crucial periods.

A further site to be explored in the Cardiff area lay on the eastern outskirts of the city at Rumney. Here, an early medieval earth and timber castle was excavated between 1978-81, over a total period of twenty months.

The castle was founded soon after the Norman conquest of this area, perhaps in the first years of the twelfth century, and was sited to protect an important crossing of the river Rhymney. It was originally a form of castle known as a 'ringwork', where a defensive bank and ditch were used to enclose a comparatively small area. In this respect it differed quite markedly from the earthen motte or mound at nearby Cardiff. To begin with, the buildings at Rumney were made from wood, including the defensive gateway to the ringwork itself. When excavated, the only indications as to the size of the internal structures were the large 'post pits' which had been used to support the upright timbers of extensive wooden frameworks. Both the gateway and a series of massive timber halls had been constructed in this way.

In the early 1270s the castle was radically transformed. The defensive ringwork bank was cut down and the interior levelled up; the castle

had lost its defensive role. A new and comfortable stone hall was constructed, and Rumney appears to have become the centre of a manorial complex for the lord of Glamorgan.

This role was, however, to be short-lived. The buildings were to be destroyed by fire, probably in the Welsh uprising of 1294, never to be rebuilt. The charred remains of the hall's roof were found to bury a hoard of silver pennies of Edward I which provided important confirmation on the date of the fire.

Rumney is now one of the most comprehensively excavated castles in the whole of Wales.

An aerial view of the excavations upon the 'ringwork' castle at Rumney. Early stages of work can be seen through a clearing in the trees. From this view it is possible to appreciate the castle's ideal position for guarding an important crossing of the River Rumney. The castle was established soon after the Norman conquest of the area and remained in use until the 1290s.

The initial gateway into the 'ringwork' of Rumney Castle is marked by a series of post pits. These show the position of two successive phases of timber gates. The metalling at the centre was no doubt a response to the continued passage of carts, horses and feet.

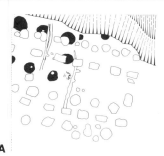

A

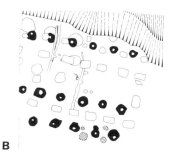

B

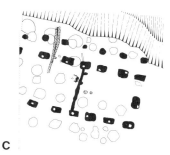

C

A series of large excavated post pits mark a succession of substantial timber halls at Rumney Castle. The accompanying plans reveal the three main phases in black, and show that the successive halls eventually had aisles. They represent the earlier phases of occupation at the site and would have supported impressive super-structures of no mean stature. The final timber hall was, however, eventually replaced by a stone construction elsewhere in the 'ringwork'.

103

9
Rescue Archaeology: Cowbridge and the West

Almost from its beginnings, the Glamorgan-Gwent Archaeological Trust has devoted a great deal of time and effort to the archaeology of the small market town at Cowbridge and its surrounding region. It is, therefore, very pleasing for us to observe that the reward for such a considerable programme of work has been an extremely interesting series of results and findings.

Although most of the detailed excavations have been undertaken in the town itself, occasionally smaller projects have been carried out in the fields and farmland of this attractive area. In the summer of 1982, for example, limited work was completed in the isolated churchyard at Llanfrynach on the western outskirts of the ancient town.

Llanfrynach lies in the shadow of the large Iron Age hillfort at Caer Dynnaf. A narrow lane separates the church from the ploughed out remains of a Romano-British farmstead, itself discovered in 1976. Landscaping within the churchyard provided an opportunity for a small excavation, hopefully to determine if the site had been occupied in the Roman period. In fact, the results proved somewhat surprising.

Parts of two large medieval buildings were uncovered, one of which appeared to be domestic, whereas the other was of some agricultural purpose. They may well have been related to the appropriation of the church by Margam Abbey during the fourteenth century, and their discovery has significant implications for a variety of buildings as yet awaiting identification in churchyards throughout South Glamorgan and further afield.

The excavation and survey undertaken at Llanfrynach has opened up many avenues for further work. The relationship between the Romano-British farmstead and later settlement, for example, is most intriguing. What is more, the cause of the disappearance or desertion of the medieval village, which is sure to have surrounded the now isolated church, presents a fascinating challenge.

Turning to the details of historic Cowbridge, it is difficult to know where to begin. So much has been achieved in a long series of excavations going back to the winter of 1977-78, with further work in 1979, a detailed full year programme in 1981-82 and completed, for the moment, with an additional six month season in 1983. All of these excavations have been completed in advance of housing and commercial developments of various kinds, and have recovered vitally important details on aspects of the Romano-British and medieval settlement, which otherwise would have been lost forever.

To begin with, the discoveries concerning the Romano-British occupation have transformed our ideas, from regarding the site as something almost negligible, to an appreciation of its true military and civilian significance.

On the military side, it has been argued for many years as to whether or not Cowbridge is the site of a missing Roman station, known from documentation as *Bovium*. Thus, during the 1977-78 excavations at 75 High Street, one of the most exciting finds was a tile stamped LEG II AUG (Second Augustan Legion), thereby providing a strong indication of a military presence. Since that time numerous other such tiles have been recovered, and have been associated with even more concrete evi-

An aerial view of the isolated church at Llanfrynach, Penllyn. Within the field, across the lane from the churchyard, lies the ploughed out bank of a Romano-British enclosure. The church itself may well overlie a site (? farmstead) of this period. It is also likely that a medieval village awaits discovery in the surrounding area. A series of interesting medieval buildings has recently been excavated within the comparatively large churchyard.

Previous Pages:

A general view of the ancient borough of Cowbridge from St Hilary Down. The town is situated at a crossing point within the Thaw valley. The hedgerows in the foreground line up with the main A48 road in the distance, and represent the alignment of the major Roman route across the Vale and through the town.

106

dence for the activities of the army at this location.

In particular, during the 1981-82 programme, a large military style bath house was excavated on the north side of the town at a site called 'Arthur John Car Park'. The building was of several main phases, with a furnace room to one end and the usual sequence of hot, cold and service rooms. The dates of its construction and use in the early second century would seem to accord well with the known movements of the army in this area.

Yet further indications have come from a site to the rear of 61 High Street where a short, but crucial, stretch of Roman ditch has been identified. Although it was impossible to excavate this fully, there is every possibility that it may have been part of the defences surrounding an auxiliary fort, and that this fort is likely to have been the missing *Bovium*.

One final piece of evidence is the recovery from a site on the extreme western end of modern Cowbridge, at 'Hopyard Meadow', of a stone statue of a lion. This lion, one of the finest pieces of sculptured stone yet to appear from Roman Wales, is likely to have been part of a funerary monument of a high ranking military or administrative official.

Following the military presence, Cowbridge continued to play an important role throughout the Romano-British period. For want of a better term, a 'small town' grew up around the military base and eventually served as a market centre for the villas and farmsteads of the surrounding Vale of Glamorgan.

A number of open fronted shops, with probable living accommodation to the rear, have been located along the present High Street. This was also the main road during the Roman era, and some of the best examples

An overall view of the excavations at 75 High Street, Cowbridge in the winter of 1977-78. The light snow cover demonstrates just one of the hazards of rescue excavation during the winter months. Despite such problems two contemporary buildings, fronting on to the main road, were found at this site and have been interpreted as Romano-British shops. They were destroyed by fire, perhaps in the third century, and replaced by a minor road heading north from the town centre. The function of the rounded pedestal in the foreground is not clear, but it may have been linked with industrial processes.

At the northern end of the bath house building in Cowbridge lay the furnace room (praefurnium). This was originally quite small, but soon after AD 120 it was replaced by a much larger room, and may well have been an attempt to combat increasing dampness at the site.

Excavations at the 'Arthur John Car Park' site, Cowbridge, reveal the footings of a distinctly military style Roman bath house. It was built around AD 100 and had been abandoned before the end of the second century. The building provides yet further evidence of a military presence at Cowbridge during the early Roman period.

have been found fronting on to this at 75 High Street. These seem to have been finally destroyed by fire around the turn of the third century.

On the northern side of the town, in the area known as the Bear Field and Bear Barn, a considerable portion of the former Romano-British settlement has now been explored. Whatever buildings were located in this area, they are most likely to have been constructed of timber, and there are strong indications in the form of large quantities of iron slag that this part of the settlement was devoted to metalliferous industrial activity.

Altogether these excavations have not only given us the probable site of the missing fort of *Bovium*, but have also provided evidence for the first justifiable 'small town' in Wales. Others will no doubt be discovered and accepted in due course.

Turning to the medieval town, some of the recent findings have been just as exciting as those concerning the Roman period. A number

Excavations at 'Hopyard Meadow', Cowbridge were initially undertaken to determine the extent of the medieval town. In fact, at least three late thirteenth to early fourteenth century buildings were discovered fronting on to the main road. It appears that the medieval built up area extended well beyond the walled town and included the entire lengths of modern Westgate and Eastgate.

Previous Pages:

Left:
The careful excavation of a 'crouched' inhumation at the 'Arthur John Car Park' site, Cowbridge. The skeleton is that of an adult male of the Roman period. Somewhere in the vicinity of the modern town, it seems likely that a substantial Romano-British cemetery awaits discovery.

Right:
The remarkable find of a beautifully carved stone lion, which appears to have been carefully placed near the terminal of a fourth century ditch at 'Hopyard Meadow', Cowbridge. The lion is probably of second century date, and is likely to have formed part of a significant funerary monument. This monument may well have been situated along the Roman roadside, near to where the lion was discovered. It provides an important indication as to the status and rank of some individuals at Cowbridge during this period.

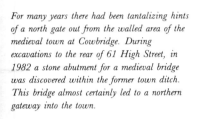

For many years there had been tantalizing hints of a north gate out from the walled area of the medieval town at Cowbridge. During excavations to the rear of 61 High Street, in 1982 a stone abutment for a medieval bridge was discovered within the former town ditch. This bridge almost certainly led to a northern gateway into the town.

of thirteenth to fourteenth century merchant shops or houses, for example, have been excavated within the walled area of the borough. However, of even greater interest was the discovery and proof of the full extent of the medieval settlement, with at least three late thirteenth or early fourteenth century structures found on the roadside at Hopyard Meadow. By the mid fourteenth century the town had almost certainly expanded to fill the entire area of both the modern Eastgate and Westgate.

In addition to the shops and houses, various sections of the defences of the medieval borough have been explored. To the rear of 61 High Street, part of an abutment for a bridge to span the town ditch has been recorded, and seems to provide confirmation of a suspected north gate into the walled town.

The results of all these rescue excavations in Cowbridge have focussed attention firmly on the very great potential of the surviving archaeology in such small market towns.

A superb aerial view of the remarkable Roman
building at Cold Knap, Barry. The building
comprised a total of 21 rooms arranged around
a central courtyard, and was probably
constructed in the late third or early fourth
century during the reign of the self-proclaimed
emperor Carausius. Its position on the coast,
with excellent views across the Bristol Channel,
begs the question of maritime association.

10
Rescue Archaeology: Barry and the South

To many people Barry will present no more than visions of a large modern town, a docks in which boats laden with bananas are common visitors, and a holiday resort to which thousands of day trippers travel by coach and train each year. In fact, nothing could be more misleading. One only has to skim the surface to see that Barry and the southern Vale of Glamorgan virtually encapsulate the entire story of South Glamorgan's Heritage.

An external veranda was constructed on the seaward side of the Cold Knap Roman building. To the right are several rooms of the building itself, whereas to the left there lies the collapsed retaining wall or portico of the veranda.

Once again, many of the rich and varied hidden secrets have recently been revealed by the spade of the rescue archaeologist. The Glamorgan-Gwent Archaeological Trust has conducted at least four major programmes of work, as well as a series of lesser projects, throughout the bounds of the modern town and its environs. The sites explored range from the Iron Age right through to the medieval period and have all produced some extremely interesting results.

Let us begin at Biglis, near Palmerstown, on the eastern outskirts of the modern settlement, where between 1978-79 the Trust explored the remains of a late Iron Age and Romano-British farmstead. The site began its history in the early first century, before the arrival of the Romans. At this time it comprised an unenclosed group of circular timber huts, similar to those known from Whitton in the central Vale. The farmsteads may have been abandoned for a while during the disruptive years around the military conquest.

By the later first century the site had been reoccupied, and was eventually surrounded by a series of palisades. In the late third century a more permanent rubble boundary bank was constructed. In all this time, however, although the occupants took on many of the trappings associated with well Romanized areas, the buildings of the farmstead never appear to have progressed beyond timber huts of various sizes.

The inhabitants of this small farmstead appear to have practised a mixed agricultural economy, where both stock rearing and corn growing were of some importance. The discovery of numerous coins on the site indicates their participation in market situations, whereas the use of well made pottery and jewellery also reveals a way of life tied closely to the new

A so-called 'corn-drying' kiln discovered in excavations at the Romano-British farmstead site of Biglis, Barry. Recent work in 'experimental archaeology' has revealed that such structures would have been inefficient in the drying of corn, and are more likely to have been used to roast grain in a brewing process.

order created by Rome.

The Biglis farmstead belongs to a group of sites now becoming quite familiar in South Glamorgan, whereas our next visit is to a large single building which has so far proved virtually unique throughout Britain. The site concerned is at Glan-y-Mor, Cold Knap, where in the summer of 1980 a remarkable story gradually unfolded. Further work was carried out in the following summer in order to glean every scrap of information on this immensely exciting find.

Indications of a Roman building at this location were first identified in 1960. During construction work on an adjacent hotel, an almost square structure was uncovered and at that time was interpreted as a Roman mortuary house. It was a further twenty years before the true picture was to be revealed.

By 1979, the site overlooking an attractive foreshore had been selected for a modern housing development. In November of that year the Trust conducted trial excavations some distance to the north of the 1960 discovery. The results proved negative, and it was not until several months of surface weathering that traces of mortared masonry were located a short distance to the south. Further trial work was undertaken which resulted in an emergency programme of full-scale excavations.

Gradually, over the next eight weeks, the remains of a large one-phase building were uncovered. The discoveries caused such excitement that, with the help of South Glamorgan County Council the Vale of Glamorgan Borough Council and the Welsh Office, the site was miraculously saved from the clutches of development and was scheduled as an ancient monument. This enabled further work to be carried out in the following year.

A suggested reconstruction of the Roman building at Cold Knap. This view from the south conveys a possible scene around the close of the third century. The veranda can be seen as an approach path in the foreground, with an almost freestanding block to the right.

The building was found to comprise a total of 21 rooms arranged around a central open courtyard. The square structure discovered in 1960 probably formed an almost free-standing tower to the immediate south-west of the main block. An external veranda was identified on the seaward side, itself fronted by a portico of some form.

Very few finds were recovered from the site, but those surviving all seem to indicate a date towards the late third or early fourth century for the main phase of occupation. This, together with its clear relationship to the sea and its important position in the Bristol Channel, all seems to suggest construction during the reign of the self-proclaimed emperor Carausius. The exact purpose of the building remains a mystery. A possible explanation is that it formed part of a *mansio*, the equivalent of a modern inn, in which case a bath house probably lay in the surrounding area. Such a complex would have been used by officials connected with government affairs. Glan-y-Mor would have provided an excellent location to await a ship on the correct tide. Alternatively, we must not overlook the strengthening of coastal defences and installations at this time. The forts at Cardiff, Lougher and possibly Neath were all refortified during the later third century, and the building at Barry may well have been linked to an overall network.

The site at Cold Knap is not only important for this unique Roman find. In addition, during the excavations a small round-cornered structure was found to overlie the earlier building. This drystone construction has since been radio-carbon dated to the turn of the ninth century, and is so far the only authenticated Dark Age domestic building in this part of Wales.

A selection of Roman coins discovered during the excavations upon the farmstead at Biglis, Barry. Not only do the coins indicate that the inhabitants of this small site were involved in a market economy, they also provide essential dating evidence on various phases of activity within the farmstead.

We can now leave the foreshore and the Roman period and move slightly north to Old Village Road, where parts of the medieval village of Barry have been explored and excavated.

The site is not far from Barry Castle, the medieval manorial centre of the de Barri family. It was first explored in 1962 when the remains of a substantial late thirteenth century peasant house were revealed. The threat of a housing development led to further excavations by the Trust in 1977, and resulted in the discovery of two more medieval peasant houses.

All three houses were initially built in the early 1200s, but were considerably altered and modified before their final abandonment in the later fourteenth century. In their later stages they were all well built constructions utilizing dressed stone, bonded together with red clay. They had beaten clay floors, and two of the houses had definite internal open hearths. Cooking would have been carried out over these hearths, and smoke would have risen to escape through the roof trusses. The roofs themselves are likely to have been constructed of thatch. Slab covered drains ran through the centre of each house and ensured relief from any excessive dampness. Moreover, despite general impressions of a squalid and dirty life in such peasant houses, the archaeological evidence from Barry suggests the interior of these buildings was kept remarkably clean. Floors must have been swept frequently to re-move domestic rubbish.

The houses belonged to a linear street settlement, extending eastwards from the castle. Their excavation represented an import-ant advancement in our understanding of shrunken and deserted medieval villages in south Wales.

Our last site worthy of some mention in the Barry area takes us back to the Iron Age. It was discovered, once again during a housing development, at Westward Corner in 1981. The remains of a substantial rock-cut ditch were recorded and it may have represented part of a previously unidentified promontory fort.

Clearly there is much of interest in the Barry area, often totally unexpected. How much more awaits discovery in this rich historic area?

A general view of a two-roomed medieval peasant house at the village of Barry. The house was first constructed in the early 1200s with round-cornered walls. It was modified and adapted over subsequent years, until it was finally abandoned in the mid to later fourteenth century. The floor of the house consisted of beaten clay, and a slabbed drain can be seen running through the centre. The reconstruction shows this (centre) and two other medieval houses which have been excavated. Their desertion indicates a process of shrinkage within the settlement in the later Middle Ages.

11

The Medieval Village of Cosmeston: A Future for Your Past

In 1954 Professor M W Beresford published a somewhat revolutionary book, entitled *The Lost Villages of England*. In it, he focussed attention upon a previously unappreciated category of archaeological site, the Deserted Medieval Village. At the time, Professor Beresford provided a gazetteer of 1,353 such sites he had been able to identify. A new survey produced in 1971 revealed that the figure had risen to 2,263, and at present the total stands at well over 2,500 with numerous examples in all parts of the country.

The initial research on this project generated considerable excitement amongst a group of professional historians and archaeologists, which in turn led to the formation of the *Medieval Village Research Group*. Each July since 1952 the *Group* has excavated part of an extensive deserted site at Wharram Percy in North Yorkshire. Such has been the subsequent interest, that numerous people, both professional and amateur, have since joined the *Group*, and excavations have been undertaken at many sites throughout England. Apart from Wharram Percy, some of the most important and revealing work has been carried out at Caldecote (Hertfordshire), Goltho (Lincolnshire), Gomeldon (Wiltshire) and Raunds (Northamptonshire), to take just a few examples. Together, the results of this work have proved remarkable and have done much to transform our ideas on medieval settlement in general.

Investigations in Wales have tended to lag behind the important advances made to the

An aerial view during the early stages of excavation upon Cosmeston medieval village. Following trial work in 1982, a long-term project has been established as a joint venture between South Glamorgan County Council and the Glamorgan-Gwent Archaeological Trust. Near the centre left can be seen the remains of an excavated dovecot in the corner of a garden enclosure. The main village excavation can be seen to the right, along the roadside.

east of Offa's Dyke. Indeed, with the recent publication (1982) of a medieval volume within the *Glamorgan Inventory* produced by the Royal Commission on Ancient and Historical Monuments in Wales, it is only just becoming apparent exactly how many deserted and shrunken village sites exist or await identification in the Principality.

In all, approximately 30 such sites have been located within the bounds of the old county and, indeed, important work was carried out in the present area of South Glamorgan during the 1960s and 1970s. In particular, medieval peasant houses were unearthed at Barry, Llandough, Lower Porthkerry, Merthyr Dyfan and Sully. Moreover, at Highlight, on the northern outskirts of Barry, as well as a survey of the deserted village, the former church and moated manor were excavated. All of these discoveries provided previously unrecorded background on medieval settlement in south-east Wales, but as yet the opportunities for a comprehensive village excavation had not arisen.

In 1977 the Glamorgan-Gwent Archaeological Trust carried out a small scale rescue excavation on the supposed site of Cosmeston Castle, near Sully in the south-eastern Vale. Unfortunately, at this time the results proved largely negative, though the findings of a documentary survey conducted as part of the project suggested strongly that the castle *and* an associated village still awaited discovery somewhere in the vicinity.

In the late summer of 1982, at the request of South Glamorgan County Council, the Trust began a further series of trial excavations within Cosmeston Lakes Country Park. Once again the work was aimed at the identification of the castle site, but more especially with an

assessment of the nature and potential of the village itself.

The project began on a site adjacent to the ruinous Cosmeston Farm Cottage (now refurbished by the County Council as a weavers' cottage), and almost immediately revealed the well preserved remains of several medieval buildings fronting on to the former main road (or village street). The presence of a deserted village at this site had finally been proved beyond doubt. Indeed, the results of this initial work were so successful, holding so much potential for full-scale investigation, that the seeds for a complete medieval village investiga-

Archaeologists at work on the reconsolidation of a medieval peasant house at Cosmeston. During the excavations the site has been open to visitors, and many of the finds displayed in a site exhibition. Such reconsolidation will eventually provide the basis for a permanent museum of medieval village life.

tion were gradually sown.

Over the winter months of 1982-83, the Trust together with the County Council planned a programme of work to last several years, which, on its completion, would probably make Cosmeston one of the most fully excavated villages in Britain. Moreover, the excavations were not to be undertaken in isolation. They were to be accompanied and complemented by a thorough documentary and archaeological survey of the entire medieval settlement pattern in the south-eastern Vale of Glamorgan. Finally, one of the most exciting aspects of the whole project is to be the creation of a living site museum. Medieval village houses and other buildings will be reconstructed, and aspects of the former way of life will be the subject of various experiments. These will range from methods of pottery production to the types of crop grown in the surrounding fields.

From documentary evidence, we now know the settlement derived its name from the Constantine or Costentin family, whose origins can be traced to Normandy, but may have arrived in this area with Robert Fitzhamon during his conquest of Glamorgan in the closing years of the eleventh century. The earliest direct reference, however, is to a Robert de Constantino, who can be identified as holding land (one fee) in south Wales in 1166. By 1304 a Thomas Costyn held the fee or manor of 'Constantinton' (Cosmeston), and the same Thomas was recorded as the lord in 1314. Soon afterwards the family appears to have lost its interest in the manor, which eventually fell to the de Cavershams and was still held by them in 1550. It is unfortunate, but we cannot be sure of the reasons for the desertion of many medieval houses. None the less, the

A fragment of a medieval 'face-mask' jug found during the 1982 excavations at Cosmeston.

poor economic conditions of the early fourteenth century, compounded by the ravages of the Black Death in 1348-49, undoubtedly played their part. Further documentary references certainly reveal a peasant population in the fifteenth century, though by 1437 the manor house itself seems to have been in ruin. The village was not totally deserted in the Middle Ages, and a number of cottages remained in use right through the post-medieval centuries.

Turning to the excavations themselves, work began in earnest during May 1983, and within a short time a large open area had been uncovered with evidence for a number of medieval structures. Principally, on the eastern side of the former village street, two medieval plots have been examined. The northern plot was found to contain an extremely interesting group of buildings, which may well have comprised a single well-to-do farmstead. Adjacent to, and parallel with, the street lay a large barn, itself separated from its associated single-roomed house to the east by a small byre or storage building. All three were built around a paved courtyard, probably during the early fourteenth century and may represent something of an expansion in the village at this time. The house consisted of low stone walls and, originally, is likely to have had a timber superstructure.

To the south of this plot, two further houses fronting on to the street have been identified. Once more their construction in stone seems to have taken place in the early fourteenth century, and their dimensions were almost identical to their neighbour. Slightly further south again, an elaborate kiln or oven has been excavated, and this could represent the village bakehouse.

THE WORK OF THE TRUST

*As well as the excavations, a permanent
exhibition of the work at Cosmeston is on
display at the site. It also includes information
on medieval settlement throughout south-east
Wales, and background detail on further projects
by the Glamorgan-Gwent Archaeological Trust.*

133

On the hillside, above the main village area, the ruins of a circular dovecot have been excavated and found to be similar in form to examples still standing at Llantwit Major and Cadoxton, Barry. Such structures were usually linked with manorial centres. The Cosmeston dovecot could have housed some 500 pairs of birds when intact, and would have been an important supply of eggs and fresh meat.

Other areas have been explored since the excavations began, and there are definite hints as to the location of the all important manor house belonging to the Constantine lords and their successors. It seems likely that this will eventually be fully recorded by the archaeologist.

Work has already progressed well with reconsolidation of the existing remains. Both the dovecot and the important farmstead group at the northern part of the site have been sympathetically restored. Further progress will be made as additional buildings are uncovered and recorded.

The work at Cosmeston represents something quite unique and should be welcomed by the people of South Glamorgan. As well as playing host to exhibitions, informative tours and even 'medieval fayres', it is clearly a new and challenging attempt to uncover more of their rich and formidable heritage.

A general view of the fully excavated farm complex on the northern part of the Cosmeston site. In the photograph the former village street ran to the left of the large tree stump, with the footings of a large barn seen running parallel to this. The clear remains of a substantial early fourteenth century house lie to the right, which was originally separated from the barn by a small byre or a buidings used to store farm implements. The suggested reconstruction views these buildings from the opposing direction, with the house to the left. Such a view will, hopefully, provide the basis for a complete rebuilding.

12
Sites to Visit

Exploring Your Heritage

The buildings, monuments and sites mentioned in this book are but a small selection of those situated throughout the area. The Glamorgan-Gwent Archaeological Trust now has almost 2000 such items on its Record for the county. The vast majority of these, however, are in private ownership, and it is necessary to seek permission before exploring the actual detail. Having said this, virtually every farm, field, village and town has something to offer.

Peering over one hedgerow, for example, might reveal the slight but clear traces of a Bronze Age barrow, whereas a short distance away there may lie the distinct mounds of a shrunken medieval village. Alternatively, numerous farm and village houses will show traces of their origin in the sixteenth and seventeenth centuries. There are hillforts and castles, churches and chapels, mansions and civic buildings, all of which can be viewed in some detail by the casual observer.

In addition, the following sites and museums have been laid out somewhat more formally for the interested visitor:

Sites

Cardiff Castle: (OS map 171, ST181766) Site of a late Roman fort and medieval castle, much modified and rebuilt in the nineteenth century.

Castell Coch: (OS map 171, ST131826) A glorious nineteenth century castle built on medieval foundations. Designed by the architect William Burges for the third Marquess of Bute.

Cosmeston Village: (OS map 171, ST277689) Site of a deserted medieval village and manorial centre. The village has been under excavation and reconsolidation since May 1983. Best visited during the Spring and Summer months, there are guided tours of the excavation and an exhibition of finds.

Dyffryn House: (OS map 171, ST096724) A large country house in Classical style built for the Cardiff shipowner John Cory in 1893. The gardens are particularly attractive.

Glan-y-Mor, Cold Knap, Barry: (OS map 171, ST099665) A unique Roman building, saved from the threat of development and excavated 1980-81. Carefully laid out with a viewing platform and interpretive details.

Old Beaupre Castle: (OS map 170, ST009721) A late Elizabethan mansion developed from a medieval castle. Famous for its magnificent inner porch constructed in 1600.

St Donat's Castle: (OS map 170, SS934678) Site of a medieval castle, enlarged and altered in the Elizabethan period and now an international sixth form college. Open with guided tours during Summer months.

St Lythans, Maesyfelin: (OS map 171, ST101723) Neolithic chambered tomb.

Tinkinswood: (OS map 171, ST092733) Neolithic chambered tomb.

Museums

National Museum of Wales: (OS map 171, ST184769) Situated within the civic centre at Cardiff it contains many of the most important archaeological finds from Wales as a whole. The prehistoric and Roman galleries have been recently refurbished and display much of great interest on South Glamorgan.

Welsh Industrial and Maritime Museum: (OS map 171, ST192745) Situated in the docks quarter at Cardiff, it provides a wealth of information on the industrial centuries.

Welsh Folk Museum: (OS map 171, ST118773) This is located in a large parkland site on the outskirts of Cardiff at St Fagans. As well as a large indoor collection on the material culture of Wales, a variety of vernacular buildings from all over the country have been reconstructed for permanent display.

The Glamorgan-Gwent Archaeological Trust is happy to supply details on other sites throughout the county. The Trust can be contacted at its headquarters in Swansea.

Select Bibliography

Suggestions for Further Reading

The quantity of literature with some bearing upon the archaeology and history of southern Glamorgan is now quite vast, and it would be impossible to provide a comprehensive list here. It is unfortunate, however, that the reader has to be somewhat discerning in order to separate what may be called 'folklore' and legend from sound historical and archaeological fact. I have tried to select some of the more recent studies, all of which carry fuller bibliographies than it has proved possible to supply here.

The list has been divided into three broad categories. The first includes a number of general works which provide important background to the specific details of South Glamorgan. This is followed by a selection of writings on the area itself, and finally there are several items such as reports and journals where there is much of direct relevance to the sites and topics covered in this book.

General Background Works

Alcock, L, *Arthur's Britain* (London 1971).

Beresford, M W, and Hurst, J G, ed, *Deserted Medieval Villages* (London 1971).

Buchanan, R A, *Industrial Archaeology in Britain* (London 1974).

Cowley, F G, *The Monastic Order in South Wales, 1066-1349* (Cardiff 1977).

Davies, W, *Wales in the Early Middle Ages* (Leicester 1982).

Megaw, J V S, and Simpson, D D A, ed, *Introduction to British Prehistory* (Leicester 1979).

Platt, C P S, *Medieval England: A Social History and Archaeology from the Conquest to 1600 AD* (London 1978).

Salway, P, *Roman Britain* (Oxford 1981).

Smith, P, *Houses of the Welsh Countryside* (Cardiff 1975).

Taylor, J A, ed, *Culture and Environment in Prehistoric Wales* (Oxford 1980).

Trinder, B S, *Making of the Industrial Landscape* (London 1982).

Wacher, J S, *Roman Britain* (London 1978).

Local Studies

John, A H, and Williams, G, ed, *Glamorgan County History, Vol V, Industrial Glamorgan* (Cardiff 1980).

Moore, D, ed, *Barry: The Centenary Book* (Barry 1984).

Pugh, T B, ed, *Glamorgan County History, Vol III, The Middle Ages* (Cardiff 1971).

Randall, H J, *The Vale of Glamorgan* (Newport 1961).

Rees, W, *Cardiff: A History of a City*, 2nd ed (Cardiff 1969).

Robinson, D M, *Cowbridge: The Archaeology and Topography of a Small Market Town* (Swansea 1980).

Spencer, M R, *Annals of South Glamorgan* (Carmarthen 1913; reprinted Barry 1970).

Williams, G, ed, *Glamorgan County History, Vol IV, Early Modern Glamorgan* (Cardiff 1974).

Williams, S, ed, *History on my Doorstep* (Cowbridge 1959).

Williams, S, ed, *Vale of History* (Cowbridge 1960).

Williams, S, ed, *The Garden of Wales* (Cowbridge 1961).

Williams, S, ed, *Saints and Sailing Ships* (Cowbridge 1962).

Williams, S, ed, *South Glamorgan: A County History* (Barry 1975).

Annual and Serial Studies

The journal *Morgannwg*, or the Transactions of the Glamorgan History Society, has appeared each year since 1957 and contains many interesting articles relating to South Glamorgan.

The *Glamorgan Historian*, edited by S Williams, was published as an annual between 1963 and 1981 and included much useful material.

The *County Treasures Survey*, produced by South Glamorgan County Council, is a mine of information on historic buildings and archaeological sites throughout the area. Each pamphlet, appearing periodically since 1976, covers a single parish or small group of parishes.

Since 1976 the Royal Commission on Ancient and Historical Monuments in Wales has published various sections of its *Inventory of the Ancient Monuments in Glamorgan*. The following parts have appeared to date:

Volume I, part i (1976), *The Stone and Bronze Ages*.

Volume I, part ii (1976), *The Iron Age and the Roman Occupation*.

Volume I, part iii (1976), *The Early Christian Period*.

Volume III, part ii (1982), *Medieval Secular Monuments, Non-defensive*.

Volume IV, part i (1981), *Domestic Architecture, the Greater Houses*.

These, together with the subsequent volumes to appear, will be indispensable to the serious student.

Finally, the Glamorgan-Gwent Archaeological Trust has produced an *Annual Report* each year since 1976-77. Many of the excavations outlined in this book are covered in more detail in these *Reports*:

1976-77 (Barry Village).

1977-78 (Coed-y-Cymdda, Cowbridge, Rumney Castle).

1978-79 (Biglis, Coed-y-Cymdda, Cowbridge, Llandough).

1979-80 (Coed-y-Cymdda, Cold Knap, Cowbridge, Rumney Castle).

1980-81 (Cold Knap, Cowbridge, Rumney Castle, Westward Corner).

1981-82 (Cosmeston, Cowbridge, Llanfrynach, Rumney Castle).

1982-83 (Cosmeston, Cowbridge, Merthyr Dyfan).

As well as accounts of excavations, these *Reports* include the results of survey work and a variety of general articles, all of direct relevance to the heritage of South Glamorgan.

Acknowledgements

The illustrative material used throughout this volume is taken directly from that used in the Canal Underpass exhibition at Kingsway, Cardiff. It has, however, proved necessary to reduce the content considerably. Many people have been involved in the technical side of producing the illustrations, but particular thanks in this respect should go to J M Daly, C A P Daly, W Lewis and T M Long.

The author and publishers would like to thank the following individuals and bodies for supplying material on pages as credited:

G Beaudette:
15 (from an original in the *Public Library J*, **3**, 1901-2), 77 (from an anonymous original)

Glamorgan County Record Office:
56-7 (reproduced from an original engraving)

Glamorgan-Gwent Archaeological Trust:
104-5, 108 (D W H Allen); 35 bottom, 49 bottom, 67 bottom, 103 centre, 125 bottom (J M Daly); 21, 22, 28, 36-7, 45, 58, 70, 135 bottom (C A P Daly); 125 top (G Dowdell); 120-1 (C L Doxsey); 18, 23 top, 24-5, 26, 40-1, 43, 50, 52, 63, 74 (B Griffiths); 49 top (B Griffiths from a scaled model by H J Thomas); cover, title-page, 12, 14, 18, 29, 34, 39 top, 40 inset, 42, 46 bottom, 81, 85, 87, 92, 93, 94, 96, 98, 99, 100 top left, 100 top right, 100 bottom, 101, 102, 103 bottom, 107, 110, 111, 112, 116, 117, 119, 122-3 (W Lewis); 103 top (K W B Lightfoot); 35 top, 48, 65, 88-9, 91, 130, 131, 133 (T M Long); 113, 114 (A G Marvell); 72-3, 115, 126, 128 top, 128 bottom, 135 top (J Parkhouse); 30, 54 top, 82 (B E Vyner)

National Museum of Wales (copyright reserved):
23 bottom, 39 bottom, 53, 66, endpapers

Royal Commission on Ancient and Historical Monuments in Wales (copyright reserved):
54 bottom, 55, 60, 61, 64, 67 (M Griffiths)

Sai Design (Bridgend):
33, 46 top (B J Williams)

South Glamorgan County Council:
86

H J Thomas:
67 top (from an original in the Glamorgan County Record Office)

University College Cardiff, Department of Archaeology:
31 (M G Jarrett); 32 (H Mason)

Welsh Folk Museum, St Fagans:
68-9, 80

Welsh Industrial and Maritime Museum:
75 top, 75 bottom, 78

Western Mail and Echo:
17

Index

List of Subscribers

The following have associated themselves with the publication of this volume through pre-publication subscription:

Stephney Amor, Swansea
Clive A Andrewartha, Hengoed
Drs M W and D H Annear, Ewenny
Mr and Mrs Gerald Beaudette, Barry
Mr and Mrs N J Brace, Rufford
Stephen Briggs, Llangwyryfon
A T Brown, Cowbridge
N G Brown, Cowbridge
Miss A M Burnet, Salisbury
Sally and Philip Carpanini, Dartington
William Carver, Abergavenny
Wendy Chaloner, Tunbridge Wells
Clwyd County Council Planning Department
Mr B R Davies, Cardiff
H R J Davies, Swansea
Melvyn Davies, Reynoldston
Robert J Davies, Swansea
Paula Dixon, Bryncoch
D E Dowdell, Swansea
G Dowdell, Swansea
John Elias, Cardiff
T T J Ellis, Swansea
Dale E Evans, Cardiff
Dr E M Evans, Swansea
Mr and Mrs G E Evans, Cardiff
Hilda and Emyr Evans, Bury
Janet Evans, Bassaleg
Muriel Bowen Evans, Trelech
Graham and Kim Falck, Magor
R J P Fisher, North Cornelly
Clive Francis, Southerndown
D P Freeman, Pontardulais
The Gibbins Family, Penarth
J K and M Greensmith, Barry
Michael W Grist, Llantwit Major
Mr and Mrs P M W Gullidge, Yate
W H Hamlin, Cardiff
T M Harold Hawkins, Bridgend
Dr D J Harris, Bishopston
Jane Hill-Kann, Llandeilo
Sir Bryan Hopkin, Aberthin
John Vivian Hughes, Port Talbot
E Jackson, Cardiff
H J and T A James, Carmarthen
Jane and Granville John, Penarth
Alec and Barbara Jones, Llanblethian
Brian Russell Jones, Pontypridd
J Barrie Jones MIEH, Barry
Mr Philip B Jones, Barry
Dr Trevor H Jones, Cardiff
W Gareth Jones, Windsor
L V Kelly, Llantwit Major

Jonathan Kissock, Swansea
Mr and Mrs S W Lane, Cowbridge
Siân Elizabeth Lewis, Swansea
Jane-Marie Llewellyn, Swansea
J F Mallon and Mrs D Mallon, Neath
Gwyn and Helen Matthews, Harpenden
Mr S R C Merrett, St Mary Church
John L S Miles, Cowbridge
Mr and Mrs F T Morgan, Cardiff
Janet C Moseley, Swansea
National Museum of Wales Library
Mr M Owen, Aberfan
Henry Owen-John, Swansea
L and E Owen-John, Churchstoke
Dr and Mrs G Page and Family, Skewen
Mr and Mrs C G Pickard, Sully
Mrs H M Powell, Sully
Peter B Pozman, York
Iorwerth Rees DipLH, Cardiff
Rhondda Museum
John Benson Roberts, Cowbridge
Mr and Mrs P D Robinson, Merthyr Tydfil
Dr David Ryan, Dinas Powys
Dr Antonio Sannia, London
H N Savory MA, DPhil, FSA, Cardiff
Mr B M See, Penarth
Steve Sell, Swansea
R G and Z W Sell, Romsey
Peter Smith, Aberystwyth
South Glamorgan County Council
    Planning Department
South Glamorgan Teachers' Centre
Jack Spurgeon, Aberystwyth
Greta M Stone (Sambrook), Bassaleg
Jonathan Taylor, Llysworney
G C and E E Thomas, Dinas Powys
Mr and Mrs Geoff Thomas, Cardiff
H J Thomas MA, FSA, Barry
Richard Thurlow, Great Malvern
D Tilley, Cosmeston
L A Toft, Swansea
Miss J E Tomsett, Merthyr Tydfil
Giuseppe Guido Tozzo, Cardiff
Mr and Mrs P Tozzo, Cardiff
Blaise Vyner, Stockton-on-Tees
K G Wake, Cardiff
Dr R P D Walsh, Swansea
Toby Warwick, Cardiff
Glanmor Williams, Swansea
N G Williams BA, Llantwit Major
The Winfrey Family, Castor
Mark and Fiona Wyatt, Swansea